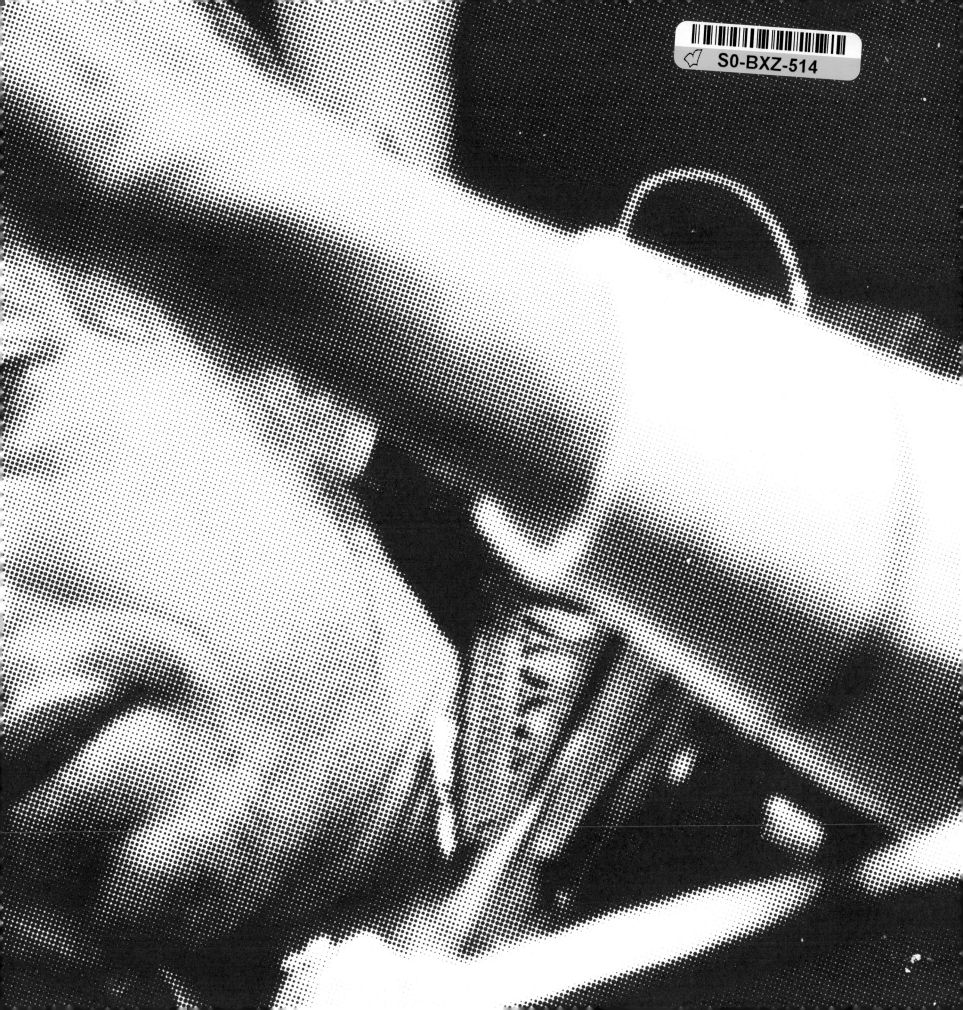

BOB DYLAN
FREEWHEELIN
HIS LIFE AND MUSIC

First Published by FHE Ltd

CAT NO: ENB0298

Photography courtesy Pictorial Press, Wikimedia Commons, Getty Images unless indicated otherwise.

Made in EU.

ISBN: 978-0-9930170-8-7

CONTENTS

On the morning of July 29th in 1966 Bob Dylan jumped onto his British-built Triumph Bonneville 650 motorcycle and rode off through the deserted roads that ran through the woods around his Woodstock home. He hadn't slept for three days, and the punishing lifestyle of the preceding years had really begun to take its toll. He was pencil thin, and photographs of him immediately prior to this particular morning show an almost haunted, distant and gaunt figure.

Cresting the brow of a hill he was blinded by the sun, and panicking, he hit his brakes. He lost control of the back wheel and came off. Injured, he lay by the side of the road with a cracked vertebrae and bad concussion. Sara (his new wife of seven months and mother to his baby son Jesse) was following safely behind in a car. That same evening as the Beatles took the stage in Candlestick Park San Francisco for what would be their last ever organised live appearance, Dylan was in hospital, where he would remain for a week. The accident happened only two months after his final controversial appearance at London's Royal Albert Hall, ending a tour during which a visibly shaken Dylan had been booed by a part of his previously idolising audience. He had famously lost his stage cool in Manchester, shouting back at the catcalls and responding to slow hand claps by telling the band to 'Play fucking loud'.

The controversy had started exactly a year before in July 1965 at the Newport Folk Festival, when the newly electrified Bob had plugged in and turned away a large part of his folk based following. Whether the audience was booing Dylan's electric set or the person responsible for unplugging him after a mere fifteen minutes is unknown. It was Dylan, of course, who had the last word when he returned to the stage with an acoustic, with a more than appropriate comment to the hostile elements in the audience by singing 'It's All Over Now, Baby Blue'.

Without doubt it was all over, and despite a deeply angered Pete Seegar, reported fights between manager Albert Grossman and Alan Lomax, and a visibly upset and shaken Dylan, it was destined to be fifteen minutes that changed the music world. Once again Dylan had led the way, and in so doing had surrounded himself in a fog of controversy that would follow him into Europe and see him booed in Paris, Sheffield, The Albert Hall, and perhaps most famously of all, in Manchester. It was here on the 17th May 1966 at the Manchester Free Trade Hall when, during a momentary lull, Keith Butler (now in his fifties and living in Canada), called from the audience to Dylan: 'Judas'.

'I don't believe you, you're a liar' Dylan fired back before launching into a lively 'Like A Rolling Stone'. As historical moments in rock music history go, this one vitriolic insult hurled at the figurehead of a musical generation stands right up there with the Stones' infamous Altamont gig in signifying the end of an era. This moment was heavily bootlegged under the incorrect assumption that it had been recorded at the Albert Hall in the capital, before it was finally confirmed that it had been the concert at Manchester in the North West.

In that one moment, an upset and hurt young fan had confirmed to the world that the times had indeed changed. Even those most animated of critics of this tour back in the mid sixties would have to agree that the passing of time has proved that Dylan had once again stepped over the parapet for others to follow. The tour took its toll, and after the storm of interviews during which he was constantly being asked to explain or justify his move away from the folk tradition that had so totally embraced him since his almost messianic arrival in the early sixties, an emotionally exhausted Dylan desperately sought some peace and quiet and returned to Woodstock to spend time with wife Sara and son Jesse.

Sara Lownds (nee Shirley Marlin Nozinsky) was born in Delaware in October 1939, making her eighteen months Dylan's senior. They married on Long Island on November 22nd 1965, and she adopted the surname Dylan rather than his birth name Zimmerman. Their marriage lasted, in legal terms, until July 1977, when their gradual separation was painfully catalogued on the 1975 album 'Blood On The Tracks'. Sara had started out as a model and been previously married to Hans Lownds, a magazine photographer who had her change her name to Sara from Shirley.

Sara had first met Dylan in Greenwich Village in 1962. They would have four children together, sons Jesse, Samuel and Jakob and daughter Anna. Dylan also legally adopted Maria, Sara's daughter from her previous marriage. She can be seen in Dylan's 1975 film 'Renaldo and Clara'

(released 1978), playing the lead female role. It would be Sara that inspired the song 'Sad Eyed Lady Of The Lowlands' that would appear on the 1966 album 'Blonde On Blonde'.

By the time of the crash Bob Dylan had produced several of the most iconoclastic albums of an era. The 1962 self titled 'Bob Dylan' album captured a fresh faced and very young Dylan displaying his full repertoire of Woody Guthrie influences, and included an original Dylan track that was a tribute 'Song For Woody'.

In 1963, 'The Freewheelin' Bob Dylan' album acted as a lighthouse to an emerging songwriting talent that few could ignore. This was an artist with not only something to say but something worth saying, and his fast emerging genius allowed him to fully communicate these protests and worldly observations to an eager and enthusiastic generation who could see that this was the poet that would lead the way for them. Legendary tracks such as 'Girl From The North Country', 'A Hard Rain's A-Gonna Fall' (a track that truly connected to a world literally living in fear of an apocalyptic end of the Cuban missile crisis), 'Don't Think Twice It's Alright', 'Masters Of War', and the masterful 'Blowin' In The Wind'. This last was written in New York and would become a flag to the youth of America.

His reputation was further underlined by some of the bravest and most confrontational lyrics to date, in anti-racism songs such as 'Oxford Town', and the anti war 'Talking World War III Blues' that captured the genuine feeling that echoed the concerns filtering through all walks of American life. As a result, his stature was already significant enough for him to be allowed to follow the Reverend Martin Luther King onto the Lincoln Memorial steps on the 28th August 1963, and to underline the legendary 'I Have A Dream' speech by performing 'Blowin' In The Wind' and 'Only A Pawn In Their Game' in front of more than two hundred thousand protestors.

In 1964 'The Times They Are A Changing' saw Dylan the temporary protest songwriter inspire and confront with finger-pointing songs such as 'Only A Pawn In Their Game', 'The Lonesome Death of Hattie Carroll' and, of course, the title track; a song that captured the feeling in the air that through music the world could change. The political turmoil was tragically illustrated when within one month of the album's release President John F. Kennedy was assassinated.

'Another Side Of Bob Dylan' quickly followed, with eleven of the tracks reportedly recorded in one amazingly productive session that gave birth to Bob Dylan's subsequent recording techniques, illustrating his desire to make albums sound real and live as though happening in your own living room rather than being over-produced. It was a technique that would shock and challenge many of the musicians that have supported

CHAPTER ONE

BOB DYLAN FREEWHEELIN HIS LIFE AND MUSIC

Dylan throughout his career. The album included 'My Back Pages', 'Spanish Harem Incident', 'All I Really Want To Do' and 'Chimes Of Freedom'. This was the start of a period of such productivity for Dylan that he was able to hand songs out to fellow musicians such as The Byrds, who famously covered 'Mr. Tambourine Man', and whose guitarist Roger McGuinn would later feature on the Rolling Thunder Tour.

A trilogy of career-defining albums followed with 1965's 'Bringing It All Back Home', 'Highway 61 Revisited' and 1966's magnificent 'Blonde On Blonde'. The first contained 'It's All Over Now Baby Blue', 'It's Alright Ma' and 'Gates Of Eden' on an acoustic side, before 'Subterranean Homesick Blues' and 'Maggie's Farm' gave a hint of what was to come on the electric side that also included 'Love Minus Zero No Limit'.

'Highway 61 Revisited' took the theme several steps further, opening with the masterpiece 'Like A Rolling Stone', then 'Tombstone Blues' and included the poetic 'Desolation Row'. It was a landmark of the musical revolution that Dylan was inspiring, and even today the album still challenges. There is tangible anxiousness to him on this album that reflects the circus that now surrounded him, leading to a feeling of urgency and amphetamine-driven edginess. He had a lot to say and seemingly couldn't write it quickly enough.

If anyone was concerned whether he could follow this, he went to Nashville and recorded the magnificent 'Blonde On Blonde'. This was the album that many argue was his Sergeant Pepper or Pet Sounds, and included 'Rainy Day Women Nos 12 & 35', 'Visions Of Johanna', 'Just Like A Woman' and a track that would earn a mention on 1975's album 'Desire'. During the song, dedicated to his wife, he tells us that he (typically) stayed up for nights in The Chelsea Hotel writing 'Sad Eyed Lady Of The Lowlands' for her. It is quite simply a classic recording and ended a period of seven of the most important albums that have ever been written.

The electrified furore of 1966 shook a folk world to its very foundations. By the time Dylan came off his motorbike on that too-sunny morning in July 1966 the relentless demands and pressure had driven him to the point of nervous exhaustion. The voice of a generation lay in a hospital bed as rumours circulated of him being disfigured or even dead.

In truth, it appears that the people simply could not get used to a world where Bob Dylan was suddenly silent, and his mysterious disappearance left a huge gap that desperately needed to be filled. Being Bob Dylan meant that when he did finally appear it would be a memorable and wholly unexpected experience. The roots of The Rolling Thunder Revue were well and truly planted on that potentially fatal day. Dylan emerged changed by the experience, stating that he saw not only his past but his future fly before him. That future would include the much-underrated

1968 country classic 'John Wesley Harding', a sprawling soundtrack of an album. The past included 'Tarantula' a speed-inspired written work he could no longer relate to, such was the change in his post-accident state of mind.

As he retreated to Woodstock, the nation continued to move towards an event at that very location that would come to represent the whole 'Times They Are A-Changing' movement. Seemingly, even in his absence Dylan could inspire a whole generation. Whatever the extent of the accident and whatever injuries Dylan suffered it gave him exactly the space he clearly needed. It quite possibly saved him, as it is clear that he could not sustain a life of staying up day after day without sleep, surviving on pills to keep going with his mind racing through soundscapes, poems and statements.

He worked on the film of the eventful 'Judas' tour that had ended just before the crash, peering at images of a Dylan that he no longer knew. He busied himself by reading through the 'Tarantula' material and working on the biographical film 'Eat The Document', which opens with him snorting an unknown substance in a Paris Hotel. But in the main he stayed out of the spotlight. Ironically his absence left him sought after to such an extent that it bordered on obsession.

During the summer of '67, as a whole movement enjoyed what is known as the summer of love, Dylan was strangely absent. Instead, he was reassessing his life, and part of that reassessment seemingly involved settling a couple of accounts. He reworked 'All American Boy' into his own retaliation against manager Albert Grossman. The song wouldn't be heard publicly for another twenty-five years. More significantly he began to record again. Also living in Woodstock at that time in the legendary house known as 'The Big Pink' or 2188 Stoll Road West Saugerties, was three fifths of The Band.

The Band, or The Hawks as they had been known, consisted of Levon Helm, Garth Hudson, Robbie Robertson, Rick Danko (d. 1999) and Richard Manuel (d. 1986). This incredible array of talent gathered in the house to start impromptu work on sessions that would finally, after many years of bootlegging, be officially released in the mid-seventies during the time of The Rolling Thunder Revue. The Band's influence on music at that time cannot be understated, and the Basement Tapes excellent double release perfectly showcases the personnel on display.

They had started life as The Hawks, a backing band for rockabilly Ronnie Hawkins, before firstly becoming Levon and The Hawks, and subsequently joining Dylan on the infamous 1965-1966 tour. It was formed of multi-talented and multi-instrumentalist musicians, boasted three lead singers and a sound that meshed country with rock and that epitomised Americana. Lead guitarist Robertson had worked with Dylan

on 'Blonde On Blonde', replacing guitarist Mike Bloomfield, and was joined on that album by Hawks colleagues Hudson and Danko.

The Basement Tapes, although not revealed to the public, contained a new Dylan and a new direction that saw him exploring the old whilst writing some new, but most importantly had him recording again. It is very much a partnership between Dylan and a band of incredible talent that meshed together to produce an absolute gem of an album. Each member explores the roots of American music at a time when the world's eyes were on the West Coast of the country. There was even room for Dylan to provide one of his most emotionally charged offerings with 'Tears Of Rage', a track that seems to illustrate why he was keeping a lower profile.

Once the sessions finished, The Band, with the influential Levon Helm back full time, broke away to make one of the most important musical documents of the era in 'Music From The Big Pink'. Dylan meanwhile conjured up a Gospel-soaked country classic in 'John Wesley Harding', an album that contained such gems as 'All Along The Watchtower', 'I Dreamed I Saw St. Augustine' and 'I Pity The Poor Immigrant', all of which would feature strongly in The Rolling Thunder Tour several years later. Both of these albums, whose seeds were sown in the basement of The Big Pink earlier that year, have been cited by many musicians of the time as being of the utmost importance in setting a standard that so many tried to follow.

Most significantly 'John Wesley Harding' introduced a calmer less wired Dylan as he explored music away from the modern world, a world that had caused him so much anxiety and pain. It also opened the door to his exploration of the spiritual with scripture-based references and gospel-tinged sounds. It was journey that would ultimately lead him on yet another trip to controversy several years later.

April 1969 saw Dylan return to the studio and emerge with 'Nashville Skyline', an album that received mixed reviews. Perhaps this was inevitable as it opens with a duet of Dylan and fellow legend Johnny Cash singing 'Girl From The North Country'. The song hardly compliments either of their reputations, and the continued Country & Western stance doesn't help. His disappointed fans reflected on the fact that where 'John Wesley Harding' had been atmospheric and almost mystical in places this album was altogether more lightweight by his standards. Despite the criticism, Dylan himself was reported as saying it was his most satisfactory release to date. On the 1st May 1969 Dylan was invited to appear on The Johnny Cash show and performed powerful and confident versions of 'I Threw It All Away' and 'Living The Blues'.

In August 1969 Albert Grossman ceased being Dylan's manager, a fact that in part may explain some of Dylan's reluctance to release the

BOB DYLAN FREEWHEELIN HIS LIFE AND MUSIC

BOB DYLAN FREEWHEELIN HIS LIFE AND MUSIC

'Basement Tapes' recordings officially, as Grossman would have profited by them. He seemed more than happy in the apparent domestic bliss that he had carved out for himself in Woodstock, a picture that he had unquestionably illustrated on 'Nashville Skyline' as he questioned his pre-crash life with songs such as 'Tonight I'll Be Staying Here With You' and the intensely reflective 'I Threw It All Away'. It is an album that, despite being largely disappointing on release has fared well in retrospect – after all it contains one of Dylan's best-known hits 'Lay Lady Lay'.

As the world descended on Max Yasgur's farm for the weekend of August 15th to 17th 1969, Dylan himself left for the United Kingdom.

The location of the Woodstock festival was no coincidence, but Dylan didn't answer the call and instead agreed to perform at the 31st August Isle Of Wight Festival instead. The promoters of the Festival, the Foulk brothers three, had relentlessly pursued Dylan to headline the second gathering, and it took six months to prize him out of Woodstock to do just that. The first festival on the small island off the south coast of England had taken place the previous year at Godshill, when San Francisco band Jefferson Airplane headlined on a bill that also included a very new T. Rex. Writing this many years later, it seems, on the face of it, strange indeed that he should agree to appear on a small island that he may have never heard of while the world watched amazed as the biggest festival in the world achieved legendary status in his own back yard.

The venue was switched to Wootton for the arrival of Bob Dylan and The Band, The Who (who had also appeared at Woodstock and would re-appear at the Isle Of Wight Festival the following year), Free, The Moody Blues and Joe Cocker. Tickets were eagerly snapped up at £3 each. The festival peaked the following year when The Who, The Doors and Jimi Hendrix appeared in front of a crowd of over half a million people. In Dylan's year of 1969, a medical post was set up for people not enjoying the powerful effects of LSD, and a whole community of temporary tents sprang up like a village that became known as 'Desolation Row'.

Bob Dylan stayed at the Forelands Farm, Bembridge and was soon visited by John & Yoko Lennon, George & Patti Harrison and Ringo & Maureen Starr. The set list was, as ever, anything but finalized, and right up until the last moment several lists handed to The Band had question marks next to them. To a rapturous welcome the white-suited Dylan and The Band took the stage. What happened next is open to interpretation. To some it was an all too brief moment in the presence of genius – to others it was the personification of disappointment.

Among the crowd most of The Beatles, The Stones, Elton John, Jane Fonda and her husband Roger Vadim and Syd Barrett's Pink Floyd attended, having all been drawn to see an icon. Dylan opened with 'She

BOB DYLAN FREEWHEELIN HIS LIFE AND MUSIC

Belongs To Me' and worked through a set that also included 'Maggie's Farm', 'Lay Lady Lay', 'Mighty Quinn', 'Mr Tambourine Man', 'Like A Rolling Stone'. The crowd's reaction to the last two songs was nothing short of electric. However only fifty minutes had passed when Dylan left the stage. He briefly returned to perform an encore, but his early departure was a huge disappointment for the massive crowd. Needless to say the short set was heavily criticised by people who really should have known better, remembering that this was his first major appearance for some time. On leaving the island the next day, he called in briefly to run through the track 'Cold Turkey' with John Lennon before flying back to the States.

Sadly, his attempt to return to the stage had ended in near disarray. Firstly he cancelled the intended release of the Isle Of Wight performance. This resulted in a bonanza for bootleggers. Despite various attempts at remixing his set, he did not want to be reminded of it, and withdrew back to Woodstock, the album unreleased, and all previous talk and plans of a tour were shelved. From the disappointment that he clearly felt, Dylan set out to dismantle all that he was seen as being.

Tired of the constant gatecrashers, voyeurs and the artistic drought that he was experiencing in Woodstock, he decided to move back to Manhattan. Quite how he felt he would escape attention in the fishbowl of The Village is not quite clear but, once decided, his wish to return to the scene he had known before the crash, took shape. By January 1970, his rationale of once again needing the vibrancy of the city resulted in him buying a town house along Macdougal Street.

Very quickly he became the victim of some quite disturbing incidents involving intrusive fans, and instead of being able to get out into the scene of the clubs, he was far too often trapped within the house. In an almost deliberate attempt to shatter some of the mania, worship and analytical dissection of all things he said and did, he went to work on one of his most controversial albums.

'Self Portrait' can be seen as the artist almost parodying himself, and in covering some unexpected material he is, perhaps, trying to push back some of the intense and unwanted scrutiny. Either way, it is, by most standards, a mystifying album. In some respects it could quite possibly have damaged many a career. When it arrived, it came in a cover depicting one of his own paintings that helped give the album its name. What he was trying to say by both the material and the cover is only really known to Dylan himself.

In retrospect, it would appear that possibly it was almost a self-destructive act to deflect some of the very unwanted attention he was always receiving. Its arrival was almost tantamount to something akin to musical meltdown. A compilation of dubious covers and lower case Dylan originals resulted in an album that had the critics positively salivating at the prospect of slaughtering him. Of course it was a job they gladly did. For example, Greil Marcus of 'Rolling Stone' famously opened his review with the line 'what is this shit?' Most wondered why the 'voice of a generation' would want to cover other people's songs in the first place, and why some of the material was dubiously selected.

Having said that, the cover of 'Copper Kettle' captures him at his unmistakable best. Many years later, we may have finally all caught up with him, and we can see an album that, although tarnished by the stinging criticism, still produces some flashes of his brilliance. Evidently the media simply could not reconcile the fact that the Dylan who had previously inhabited New York had changed almost beyond recognition. If they had looked a little deeper, they would have seen that, hidden within the album were several originals from sessions recorded in March 1970 that indicated that he had once again found inspiration. 'It Hurts Me Too' & 'Alberta' (both versions) sit strongly among this strange statement.

Stung and hurt by the vitriolic response to 'Self Portrait', Dylan dipped into the studio once again and came out with 'New Morning'. The sessions were conducted in New York just as 'Self Portrait' hit the racks. It was released a mere four months later. It is an album, once again, that projects a warmth of continued contented domesticity as Dylan reflects on being a father whilst trying to escape the craziness that had nearly destroyed his life back before the crash. In complete contrast to 'Self Portrait', 'New Morning' was full of original material. The album starts with 'If Not For You', a song famously covered by good friend George Harrison (d. 2000) on his triple 'All Things Must Pass' set. The introspective 'Sign On The Window' is a truly standout track and would have been so in any Dylan set.

Although still a little weak by his own impossible standards, 'New Morning' was heralded as a return to form. The album ends with a strong indication of where Dylan's thoughts were heading with the deeply inspirational 'Father Of Night'. The relative warm reception that 'New Morning' had enjoyed almost prompted Dylan to go back on stage, and he had even commenced rehearsals with Al Kooper and Harvey Brooks amongst others. Sadly, the intended live dates did not materialise. In another significant development, Dylan parted company with Albert Grossman, finally ending their partnership on July 17th 1970. Meanwhile, the book 'Tarantula', dating from before the crash, finally started to appear in bootleg form, becoming an underground cult item.

1971 and 1972 saw Dylan entering his quietest period to date. It was an era that did not produce any new albums and rumours of his writing block continued unabated.

BOB DYLAN FREEWHEELIN HIS LIFE AND MUSIC

CHAPTER ONE

BOB DYLAN FREEWHEELIN HIS LIFE AND MUSIC

During this period, on 1st August 1971, he responded to a call from George Harrison and appeared for charity at New York's Madison Square Garden in The Concert For Bangladesh. His appearance there was in the balance right up until the time Harrison ended a beautiful version of 'Here Comes The Sun' from The Beatles' 'Abbey Road' album, and looked hopefully over to see if Dylan was actually going to come on to the stage or not. Seemingly, the previous night at the sound check, nerves had got the better of him, and he had said that he just couldn't do it. With a tangible sense of relief Harrison saw him anxiously waiting in the wings. 'I'd like to bring on a friend of us all, Mr. Bob Dylan', he announced.

The response was immediate. Dylan took the stage looking nervous but inspired, wearing a denim jacket, and after a few moments adjusting the height of the microphones, he launched into a superb 'A Hard Rain's A- Gonna Fall'. The New York audience was in raptures. His twenty minutes on stage consisted of pre-crash material, and he even responded to Harrison's request to perform 'Blowin' In the Wind', a track of total relevance to the occasion, much to the delight of the ex-Beatle. The audience reaction to a now rare public airing of this classic was one of pure emotion.

When he left the stage, the resulting standing ovation was a genuine and heartfelt response to having him back. The Concert was released as a triple box set and included sets from George Harrison himself, Ravi Shankar, Ringo Starr, Leon Russell (whom Dylan had briefly worked with earlier in the year on 'When I Paint My Masterpiece'), Badfinger's Pete Ham (d. 1975) and Billy Preston (d. 2006). Dylan's set was given a full side of vinyl as he ran through 'A Hard Rain's A-Gonna Fall', 'It Takes A Lot To Laugh/It Takes A Train To Cry', 'Blowin' In The Wind', 'Mr. Tambourine Man' and 'Just Like A Woman'. Backed by half the Beatles and Leon Russell, the result is somewhat patchy, but most importantly it confirmed to those lucky enough to witness the event that he was not only alive and well but could still dominate, albeit in this case unwittingly, any event amongst any company.

One more appearance followed that year when he turned up at The Band's New Years Eve performance, turning in a superb 'Down In The Flood'. Despite the obvious chemistry between Bob Dylan, Robbie Robertson, Rick Danko, Richard Manuel, Levon Helm and Garth Hudson, and the rapturous response the appearance had ignited, he did not take up the offer of more live concerts. Instead, he busied himself releasing another piece of Dylan controversy, the single, 'George Jackson', dedicated to the late black activist who had recently died whilst serving a prison sentence.

When Dylan went to see Allen Ginsberg's poetry recital at Greenwich

Village, it started an experimental project of recording improvised poetry that sadly sounded better in theory than in reality, with the intended album not achieving release. Ginsberg, who died in 1997, would later work with Dylan again during the Rolling Thunder Revue. Several more ad hoc appearances followed, such as his unannounced contribution to a John Prine gig in New York. (Prine was largely unknown at the time.)

In July 1972, Dylan was in the audience at New York's Madison Square Garden as Elvis returned from his lost years. Later that year he was also spotted at a Rolling Stones concert at the same venue. These two concerts may have acted as the inspiration that reactivated his own desire to perform live again. Firstly, though, Dylan had to go to the depths of Mexico to begin a comeback in an altogether different direction.

It was a long, quiet, three-year gap before he emerged rather strangely alongside James Coburn (Garrett) and Kris Kristofferson (Billy) on the set of Sam Peckinpah's (d. 1984) movie 'Pat Garrett and Billy The Kid'. Dylan had been sent the script and wanted to write the soundtrack to it. There was no better person to do that of course, despite Peckinpah's original insistence that Roger Miller (d. 1992) should write it.

Peckinpah had quite a reputation for bizarre behaviour, but Dylan, a film buff, knew of his work and eventually asked if there might be a cameo role for him to fill. Pat Garrett's own memoirs referred to a person known only as 'Alias' – it proved the perfect role for him. Peckinpah, meanwhile, needed convincing to take a chance on a singer that he barely knew of until he heard Dylan's already prepared track 'Billy'. Visibly affected, he immediately offered him the role.

The cast convened to Durango, Mexico where a series of mishaps, fights, typically paranoiac behaviour by the hard-drinking director and cast, equipment malfunctions and monetary problems, made each day an unpredictable event. 'Alias', meanwhile, had been all but left off the page until his first scenes showed the director just what a charismatic presence he had on hand. When Dylan completed his perfectly pitched soundtrack for the movie in Los Angeles and the album was finally released, it resulted in a much-overlooked masterpiece among the Dylan catalogue. To capture the death scene of the sheriff in the film Dylan wrote 'Knocking On Heavens Door' and in doing so produced one of his most memorable tracks ever.

When Dylan left Columbia for Asylum Records, his old label released what was little more than a collection of outtakes and discarded tracks dating back to the 'Self Portrait' and 'New Morning' sessions under the unimaginative title 'Dylan' (1973). It was instantly forgettable, which is exactly what Dylan did as he began to work on what would become the following year's 'Planet Waves'.

BOB DYLAN FREEWHEELIN HIS LIFE AND MUSIC

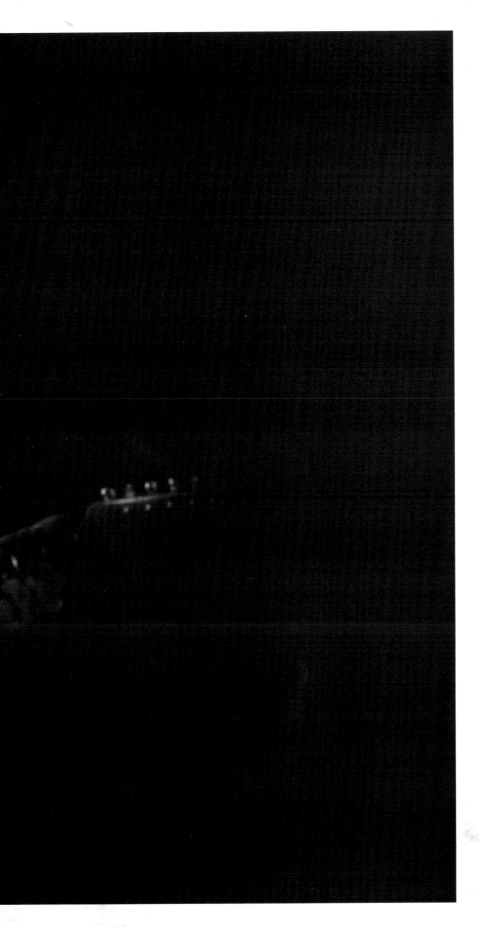

The apparent domestic contentment that he had craved, thrived upon and was clearly inspired by since the motorbike crash, was slowly derailing. During attempts to rebuild his relationship with Sara, they had visited California, and soon after in the spring of 1973 they took a lease on a house in Malibu. It was a period that saw him working once again with California-based Roger McGuinn of The Byrds, continuing a relationship that continued into The Rolling Thunder Revue.

Meanwhile, The Band had enjoyed a hugely successful concert at Watkins Glen in front of three hundred thousand appreciative fans. Soon after, Robbie Robertson, now eager to get down to the business of producing new music, arrived in Malibu and sought out Dylan. The conflict between the need to go out on the road and returning to the life that had nearly destroyed him and his marriage was now relentless. Sara knew exactly what life on the road could do to Dylan and desperately attempted to keep him safely ensconced in domesticity.

The result of the collaboration with Robertson and The Band in Malibu was the 1974 album 'Planet Waves' recorded in just three days. It remains the only ever studio album from the partnership. Kicking off with the lively 'On A Night Like This' it moves into altogether darker territory with the wonderfully evocative 'Going, Going, Gone'. Famous for including two different versions of 'Forever Young', written for his son, it moves through the disturbing self examination of his marriage to Sara with the track 'Dirge', before ending on a contradictory note with 'Wedding Song'.

Dylan could resist the desire no more and returned to the road. The accompanying tour was captured superbly on the live album 'Before The Flood', complete with The Band recorded in the huge venues brought about by an almost maniacal stampede for tickets. The album is a must for fans of Dylan or The Band as it fully captures the power of them together, and once again proves beyond any doubt that the collective musicianship among The Band was second to none.

The tour kicked off in Chicago during the first week of 1974 in front of nearly twenty thousand fans. As Dylan sang the line 'Even the President of the United States sometimes has to stand naked' (from 'It's Alright Ma'), it perfectly captured the mood of a country awash with the Watergate scandal. The tour was a massive success both commercially and in the fact that Dylan had once again stepped out onto the world stage and proved to everyone, including himself, that he could still do it at the highest of all levels. In the words of the Woodstock anthem performed by Crosby, Stills and Nash, it had been a long time coming. The live album 'Before The Flood', taken predominantly from the last show of the tour in Los Angeles, proved to be a massive-selling hit as well. The tour ended with Dylan safely reunited with Sara. It was hard to tell who was the most relieved.

CHAPTER TWO

Once the 1974 tour was, over the gaps that had opened within Dylan's marriage were becoming insurmountable. The appearance of Ellen Bernstein, who worked for Columbia Records, in his Malibu-based life, finally signalled the end. Ironically, the sadness and pain that signalled the end of his marriage to Sara would result in one of the most priceless albums of his career.

Tracing the roots way back to that fateful morning when he had slammed on his brakes and lost control of his motorbike, the subsequent era in Dylan's life resulted in several peaks and some lows, but nothing could have prepared us for 'Blood On The Tracks'.

Ironically it would be another coming off the rails that resulted in his most powerful album since his arrival had heralded a new dawn. Agreeing to folk singer Phil Ochs' (d. 1976) request to help him with a New York-based concert to highlight the plight of the political situation in Chile, where the Socialist Government had been overthrown, and his appearance there several days later, illustrates his rekindled desire to perform.

This resulted in him staying, once again, in New York for the spring of 1974, this time as a guest of Russian-born artist Norman Raeben (d. 1978) in his studio in Carnegie Hall. Dylan himself describes Raeben as a huge influence on him at that time and credits him with his dramatic return to songwriting. He also says that meeting him resulted in such a change in his outlook that Sara could no longer relate to him. Dylan spent two months doing little more than visit Raeben on a daily basis for lessons on art, life and discovery.

These lessons were to have a profound effect. Raeben helped to lift the fog of the writing amnesia that Dylan had felt that he had been suffering since the crash. Dylan has been quoted as saying, 'he taught me how to see'. Significantly, he began to write lyrics that explored Raeben's concept of 'no time'. He says of his teacher, 'you've got yesterday, today and tomorrow all in the same room and there's very little that you can't imagine doing'.

The album 'Blood On The Tracks' has been described by Dylan on the notes to his biography as 'I was just trying to make it like a painting where you can see the different parts but then you also see the whole of it. With that particular song (Tangled Up In Blue) that's what I was trying to do. With the concept of time and the way the characters change from first person to the third person and you're never quite sure if the third person is talking or the first person is talking. But as you look at the whole thing, it doesn't really matter.'

'Blood On The Tracks' makes Dylan's earlier 1971 track 'When I Paint My Masterpiece' uncannily relevant. The song has him searching for an inspiration as he aches to return to write his masterpiece. 'Blood On The Tracks' was undoubtedly that, and even after thirty or more years regularly appears in polls of the most influential and 'best' albums of all time. Whatever Raeben unlocked in the Dylan psyche helped release him from the smog of uncertainty, and he emerged with a collection of songs that form a truly remarkable study of pain and anguish. It is intensely personal, and the listener cannot help but feel the torment echoing through each track. Dylan had finally produced his masterpiece.

Behind the scenes, he was spending more and more time with Ellen and their collective children in Minnesota, where he would write and paint. Although it represented a happy period in his life, he was still suffering from the fallout of the break up with Sara. The writing had Dylan peering back at the troubled times and the agony of the end of a relationship that had once been his whole life. As he opened up each emotion that such a breakup can ignite, he captured some of the most moving moments in a rush of magical inspiration and insight.

His present life was equally exposed with the track to Ellen, 'You're Gonna Make Me Lonesome When You Go'. It was an album that saw Dylan the poet, the painter, the lover, the artist, the storyteller, the vulnerable and all the other elements that make the man come together to reveal the tortured genius within. He even takes us back further and tells of relationships past that still haunt and taunt him. In another time and in another place it was another relationship that may have worked, and the song 'Simple Twist Of Fate' (clearly written for long lost love Suze Rotolo) (Susan Elizabeth Rotolo b. 1943) tells of a deeply held sadness over the

CHAPTER TWO

way it had all ended.

'Blood On The Tracks' is, however, centred on the end of his marriage to Sara, and despite being musically inspiring and lyrically epic, the result is sadness personified. It took a brave man to wear his heart on his sleeve so publicly knowing that, as with any Dylan album, every word, every clue and every note would be intensely and mercilessly analysed. It can be both inspirational and uncomfortable, but the landscapes it paints will haunt and strike many relevant chords within people who have experienced similar pain.

Being Bob Dylan, of course, meant that any move was met by intense media speculation, and just such a circumstance ignited the anger that resulted in one of his most memorably intense tracks, 'Idiot Wind'. It was penned just as the album was taking shape; there was misguided coverage in the press over the causes of his breakup with Sara. The anger, the disgust and contempt for these intrusions can be heard when he almost spits the first lines to 'Idiot Wind' – 'Someone's got it in for me, they're planting stories in the press, whoever it is I wish they'd cut it out quick but when they will I can only guess' (lyrics by Bob Dylan).

As if the pain of the separation wasn't enough, he had to suffer the continued invasion from misguided and ill-informed journalists. You cannot help but wonder whether he regretted his return from the 'missing years' and from a time when he busied himself with raising his family and being out of the intensity of the spotlight. The artist in him, however, had to have a creative outlet, and once he had returned, he was once again the focus of some of the most invasive scrutiny that for the likes of ordinary people is impossible to imagine. It was almost as if his every utterance was a culturally significant message to the people, the politicians or the world. His growing disbelief in the way the world had begun to view him can be seen in some of the earlier interviews, during which his shyness in front of the glare of endless questioning becomes apparent. By the end of the 1966, he had looked like a man on the edge of breakdown. 'Blood On The Tracks' tells us more about the man than any of these meetings with the press ever did.

The album opens with his masterpiece 'Tangled Up In Blue'. Inspired in its approach by his teachings from Norman Raeben, it is a wonderfully intricate piece. It is not merely a song; this is a painting, a screenplay, a book, a poem and a soundscape, deep in both texture and imagery. Every word on this album means something, every line paints an image and every track is an incredible, deeply personal journey into the soul of the writer. Quite simply the track is huge. The wounds can actually be felt and every conceivable emotion experienced by anyone who has lost someone is explored.

Dylan himself gives an insight into where the album is taking us with the line in the song during the fifth verse of seven where he has been handed a book of poems written by a thirteenth century Italian poet, when he says, 'every one of them words rang true and glowed like burning coal, pouring off of every page like it was written in my soul from me to you. Tangled up in blue.' These lines seem to capture, in essence, the whole soul of the album and as the work unwinds like an epic poem it can be seen that every word does indeed ring true. The track shifts from present to past, from first and then briefly into third person as he delves into seemingly unconnected abstract events from his life with Sara. As with many Dylan tracks you can see the events and feel an understanding of the people therein, such is the imagery he somehow conjures into the words of a song.

The album deftly moves from this epic opening into a track about an altogether different relationship from an earlier time. One of the saddest songs ever written reminds us of the eggshell that is any relationship. This was his lost love of Suze Rotolo (d. 2011) from a time back in New York, way before the crash, when Dylan was setting out on a journey that would see him achieve a status way beyond either of their imaginings.

Suze achieved immortality as the girl linking Dylan's arm on the New York City based cover of 'The Freewheelin' Bob Dylan' back twelve years earlier in 1963. She also achieved the same through the lyrics of this song. She was born and lived in Queens, a suburb of New York City, and Suze was often credited as supplying some of the political awareness in the newly arrived Bob Dylan.

A devotee of Bertolt Brecht (d. 1956) the German-born Socialist Poet and Dramatist, it was Suze who visited Cuba in 1964 at a time when it was illegal for American citizens to do so. Based in New York, Suze Rotolo worked as an artist and teacher and was credited as helping to inspire the poet and artist that existed within the young Bob Dylan. She also inspired many of Dylan's earlier works such as the painfully honest 'Ballad in Plain D' from the 1964 'Another Side Of Bob Dylan' album. But it is this song about their subsequent breakup and what that clearly meant to him that fully captures the intensity of his love for her.

By 1972 she had married film editor Enzo Bartoccioli. This is, therefore, the story of two young people who had so much going on in their lives that it would challenge anyone to stay together during it. Their time together went from being one of folk clubs and the intimacy of the New York Village scene to sudden worldwide fame, attention and all the pressure that it brought with it. As Dylan moved on, it was Joan Baez, later very much a part of The Rolling Thunder Tour, that would provide some stability, albeit temporarily, for him.

'A Simple Twist Of Fate' sadly recounts the story largely in the third person peering in on the scenes unfolding. Then, with the gift he had so superbly utilised in 'Tangled Up In Blue', the song shifts to the first person: 'I remember well', with such deeply reflective lines such as 'I still believe she was my twin, but I lost the ring. She was born in the spring but I was born too late, blame it on a simple twist of fate'. The whole song is delivered with such intimacy and is one of the best examples of Dylan's singing from among the galleries of his work both before and after. The excellent and ultimate Dylan biography, 'Behind The Shades Take Two' by the remarkable Clinton Heylin (Penguin Books), recalls that one night in London in 1981 he actually forgot himself and sang 'Suze and the way she talks'.

The next track is, if anything, even more painful and has Dylan in deeply remorseful and reflective mood. 'You're A Big Girl Now' is Dylan looking back at Sara and trying to come to terms with life without her and her life without him. It is pain personified and the wounds are deep indeed. Pleading one moment, trying to accept the next, it ends with him telling us of how he is not coping in the aftermath of the death of his marriage. 'I'm going out of my mind, with a pain that stops and starts, like a corkscrew to my heart, ever since we've been apart'. Sadly too many of us know exactly what he is saying.

There is a deep and frighteningly obvious anger to the next track, 'Idiot Wind', not only in the epic scale of the lyrics but the way he delivers them. Almost spitting contempt at the players within his life, he finally turns the anger against himself by summarising: 'we're idiots babe, it's a wonder we can even feed ourselves'. One standout line captures something of what being Dylan must feel like when he says: 'I haven't known peace and quiet for so long I can't remember what it's like'.

Possible and probable targets spring to mind, but only the writer himself can fully unlock the clues contained within. Clearly once again he turns his anger on the break down of his marriage but it is also clear that we all feature in there somewhere, and anyone that has attempted to write anything about him, myself included, is a potential target of his frustration. After all, only Bob Dylan knows Bob Dylan. After all, he must have spent his life reading reams of ill-judged and ill-informed guesswork by people trying to see inside his head and heart. Even Sara, the woman who without doubt knew him best, is not spared the gunfire when he says: 'Even you, yesterday, you had to ask me where it was at. I couldn't believe after all these years you didn't know me better than that, sweet lady'.

This is uncomfortable listening and Dylan does not spare his words.

DYLAN IN COLOUR

BOB DYLAN FREEWHEELIN HIS LIFE AND MUSIC

BOB DYLAN FREEWHEELIN HIS LIFE AND MUSIC

BOB DYLAN FREEWHEELIN HIS LIFE AND MUSIC

BOB DYLAN FREEWHEELIN HIS LIFE AND MUSIC

BOB DYLAN FREEWHEELIN HIS LIFE AND MUSIC

BOB DYLAN FREEWHEELIN HIS LIFE AND MUSIC

BOB DYLAN FREEWHEELIN HIS LIFE AND MUSIC

In fact the song was morphing with every new time he played it. His notebook for the Blood On The Tracks album contained some seventeen songs in total, of which ten would finally make the cut. At one point, Dylan had once again approached guitarist Mike Bloomfield, who had appeared on 'Highway 61 Re-Visited', but the session ended in disarray and bad feeling.

Before his death in San Francisco in 1981, Bloomfield remembered the session as Dylan playing one song after another nonstop without giving him any time to pick up on what was expected from him. He had asked Dylan if he could tape at least some parts so that he could properly learn and build the guitar parts but had received a look of suspicion about his motives that had surprised him.

Meanwhile Dylan had returned to Columbia Records, a fact that his relationship with employee Ellen Bernstein had nothing to do with. The sessions for the album were finally held on the familiar ground of A & R Studio on Seventh Avenue, the scene of several of his earlier albums. The album was produced by Dylan himself and was engineered by Phil Ramone.

Ramone has since gone on to achieve more than a dozen Grammy Awards in a career that has seen him work with such diverse talents as The Rolling Stones, Elton John, Barbara Streisand, Paul McCartney, BB King, Luciano Pavarotti, Frank Sinatra and Ray Charles among many others. He had previously worked with The Band, engineering their 1969 eponymous album and 1972's 'Rock Of Ages' before working with Dylan and The Band on 1974's 'Before The Flood'.

The sessions began with multi-instrumentalist Eric Weissberg (who has subsequently worked with Billy Joel and Art Garfunkel among others) and his Deliverance band backing the tracks as Dylan worked through them without notes or charts for his fellow musicians. Once again, Dylan typically attempted to capture the immediacy of the recordings and seemed indifferent to mistakes made along the way. Nine songs were recorded in this way, along with 'Deliverance', but of these, 'Call Letter Blues' was not up to scratch, and was dropped from what would become the final album.

The next day the sessions resumed, but only bass player Tony Brown was asked to come back. Three songs were captured that day: 'You're A Big Girl Now', 'Shelter From The Storm' and 'You're Gonna Make Me Lonesome When You Go'. For the next session keyboard player Paul Griffin, who had worked with Dylan before, joined Brown. This session saw takes of 'Buckets Of Rain', 'If You See Her Say Hello', 'Simple Twist Of Fate', 'Tangled Up In Blue' and another track called 'Up To Me', which was finally removed from the album set.

Columbia was making plans for the release of the album when Dylan suddenly changed his mind. Unusually for Dylan he had decided to record more than half of the album. This took place at the end of December in Minneapolis with local guitarist Kevin Odegard (who was then employed as a brakeman on the railway), stand up bass player Billy Peterson (best known for work with The Steve Miller Band), keyboardist Gregg Inhofer, and Bill Berg on drums. When the session resumed, Dylan added mandolin player Peter Ostroushko (subsequently a successful solo artist who has also worked with Emmylou Harris and Willie Nelson) and Jim Tardoff, a banjo player, to the ad-hoc line up.

On the 30th December, this line up re-recorded 'If You See Her Say Hello', 'Lily Rosemary and The Jack Of Hearts' and 'Tangled Up In Blue'. Also, unusually for Dylan, who by now was renowned for his lack of structure in the studio, preferring the music to evolve rather than be over-produced, the album was finally released with a generous amount of overdubbing. It became clear that the material he had written was of significant importance to him. Sadly and unjustly, the Minneapolis musicians did not appear on the credits for the album, as Columbia had already printed the cover in anticipation of an earlier release date. It is an injustice and omission that the Minneapolis musicians have been actively trying to change ever since.

'Idiot Wind' would always be a hard track to follow but this is managed with perfect balance with the track 'You're Gonna Make Me Lonesome When You Go'. It is altogether more upbeat and yet still masks the underlying sense of regret and acceptance of the inevitable. Apparently this was written around his relationship with Ellen Bernstein. It is a lovely piece of poetry, rich with one-liners and leaves the listener in no doubt whatsoever about his warmth of affection for her. It becomes clear, though, that if the chance came to go back to Sara and his family he would take it, and his time with Ellen would end; however, it is obvious through these lyrics that she would never fade from his affections.

Restoring his faith in love, Ellen had clearly been exactly the right person at the right time in his life, and her love and understanding is warmly acknowledged. This is a wonderful piece, capturing the joy in a new relationship whilst sadly acknowledging it's fragility, and ends with him acknowledging that he will never forget their time together. It is a Dylanesque conundrum that whilst desperately trying to save his marriage and acknowledging that it probably would not happen in such a public way, he also includes within that outpouring his relationship with Ellen. It's inclusion highlights that the artist is really wearing his heart on his sleeve and is being totally honest with the listener. This is indeed an album where 'every one of them words', does in fact, 'ring true'.

'Meet Me In The Morning' is soulful, almost minimalist blues delivered in perfect keeping within the sorrow of the album. This time, the loneliness is pitifully exposed as the album continues to explore and acknowledge every aspect of every emotion contained within a breakup. There has never been another songwriter who was able to come up with the screenplay that is 'Lily, Rosemary and the Jack Of Hearts'. Within one verse, you know and are interested in the characters, can see the setting and can follow the sixteen verses over nearly nine minutes as if you are in the cinema watching the story unfold. It is, fittingly, a tale of betrayal and love, therefore complimenting the album's overall scope, delivered in an upbeat country style that perfectly paves the way for the intensely personal 'If You See Her Say Hello'.

It almost feels like an intrusion listening to this song, and Dylan's voice has never sounded so genuinely emotional or pleading. Yet the song is directed at the listener as he pleads for one last contact. This sounds like the song wrote itself as it literally pours out of him as he tries to accept the inevitable. Never has he written anything as sad as this before or since. The vocals are sensitively underpinned by a superbly chosen mandolin as his voice almost breaks with the strain. To write, develop and perform a song like this in a studio environment is unquestionably further evidence of genius. It may have been written by a world famous, acclaimed songwriter, but it is relevant to anyone who has parted from a loved one.

Written months later as the feelings linger among the memories of a shared but flawed past, it tells us that, yes, we would all change parts of our lives and, yes, we all know the scenes by heart; never has a song so perfectly captured the longing and desperation that is separation.

Within a stroke we are taken back in time again as 'Shelter From The Storm' opens with 'It was in another lifetime'. It is a weary sounding Dylan that takes us on another epic journey through the scenes of his past. In any other set this would deserve to be a standout track, and taken in isolation it is yet another example of song writing in its highest form. Within this set it becomes part of a whole, with the 'whole' being an album of extraordinary brilliance.

'Buckets Of Rain' ends an unforgettable release with a superbly produced track, complete with a clean and simple acoustic arrangement over yet more revealing lyrics. The track that had to be left off for purely timing reasons was 'Up To Me', which later appeared on 1985's set 'Biograph'. Its non appearance had nothing to do with any lack of quality, but was probably chosen for its use of the same chord sequences as 'Shelter From The Storm'. Once again this track could have

sat quite impressively within any number of album listings, and its 'loss' until released some ten years later was unfortunate and acts as a perfect illustration of the quality of material that was being written at the time. The Dylans temporarily reunited in 1975 and tried to heal their wounds. Whether anything contained within 'Blood On The Tracks' helped that along can only be guessed by us on the outside, but, sadly, they were destined to go through the whole painful process again, and spent the next three years parting, this time seemingly forever.

Dylan went to visit the South of France, a trip arranged to coincide with his 34th birthday, and planned it in the hope that Sara might join him there. However, this was not to be the case, and instead, he spent his time with artist David Oppenhein, who had painted the rear cover of 'Blood On The Tracks' at his house in Savoie. At least one track, 'One More Cup Of Coffee' that would eventually appear on his next album 'Desire', was inspired during this time.

Significantly he also spent time reading boxer Rubin 'Hurricane' Carter's autobiography: 'The Sixteenth Round: From Number 1 Contender to #45472'. Carter had been convicted for his alleged part in the triple murder on June 17th 1966 in the Lafayette Bar in Paterson, New Jersey, of bartender Jim Oliver, customer Fred 'Cedar Grove Bob' Nauyoks and Hazel Tanis, who died a month after the shooting.

A fourth person, Willie Marins, had also been shot, losing an eye in the incident. Convicted alongside John Artis, both men had been sentenced to life imprisonment. Up until his conviction, 'Hurricane' Carter had been enjoying a reasonably successful boxing career, peaking in December 1963 when he defeated the highly ranked Emile Griffith, knocking him down twice in the first round and winning by a technical knockout. Carter was then ranked third in the middleweight world, beating future heavyweight champion Jimmy Ellis along the way.

In truth his career had taken a few backward steps, firstly in his defeat to Joey Giardello and then in the rankings, by losing four out of five fights in 1965 against fellow contenders, culminating in a one-sided beating at the hands of Dick Tiger. The chief witnesses in the murder trial were made infamous in Dylan's subsequent track 'Hurricane', and became household names as the controversy grew through appeal after subsequent appeal. Arthur Bello and John Dexter Bradley, both small time New Jersey criminals, testified that they saw Carter and Artis with guns outside the bar on the night in question. At the time of the incident, Bello and Bradley had been busy committing a nearby break in. A further witness was one Patricia Valentine (Miss Patty Valentine in the song), who testified to seeing the black men leave the scene by getaway car. At the time, the book was released there was an increasing call for a

retrial, as it became apparent that there were several gaping holes in the conviction.

The story clearly captured Dylan's imagination and he would go on to write a protest song that would become part of the whole process of gaining a retrial for the two men. Bello and Bradley withdrew their original testimonies, and eventually, the New Jersey Supreme Court granted Carter and Artis a hearing. In 1982, seven years after Dylan had read the book and after several hearings, appeals and retrials, the two were once again sentenced to life imprisonment.

Following a further move in 1988, the state made the decision not to hear the case again and both men were released. Artis was quickly convicted the following year and spent more time in prison, but Carter, whose boxing career had ended with his conviction, moved to Canada where he worked as a motivational speaker having also been executive director of The Association of the Wrongly Convicted. Carter died in 2014.

In 1999, nearly a quarter of a century after Dylan had made the story famous with 'Hurricane', Denzel Washington starred in a film by the same name. Dylan was destined to meet with Carter when on December 5th he went to see him at the low security establishment of Clinton State Prison where he performed several songs before Carter himself took the stage to speak to the press.

Meanwhile on 26th of June 1975, a double album version of 'The Basement Tapes' was finally released, eight years after the sessions. The main mover in the project was The Band's guitarist Robbie Robertson. There were several surprising omissions, such as Dylan's 'Sign Of The Cross' and 'I Shall Be Released', but in general it was an excellent selection that fully captured what the sessions had been about. On returning from France, whilst attempting reconciliation with Sara, Dylan was often sighted in and around his old territory of The Village in New York, where he began to witness a whole new movement with bands such as The Ramones, Television and The Patti Smith Group. Dylan greatly admired what was being touted as a female version of him and liked her whole approach to performing. Pretty soon he was working on ideas to form his own loose group of travelling musicians.

In New York he had met up with some of the musicians that would feature strongly in the Rolling Thunder Revue, among them Ramblin' Jack Elliott, Rob Stoner and old friend Bobby Neuwirth. Fellow Woody Guthrie devotee Jack Elliott had been in and around the scene in New York for some and was a renowned country artist of some standing. His influence on the early Dylan was self-evident.

Now well into his late seventies, Elliott's 1995 album 'South Coast', which represented his first output in over twenty years, won a much-appreciated Grammy Award. Multi-instrumentalist Rob Stoner had also been around The Village for a while before Dylan saw him playing bass with Jack Elliott.

Stoner (born Rothstein) also had his own band known as 'Rockin' Robin and the Rebels' and had first crossed paths with Dylan back in 1971 in San Francisco, and again two years later in 1973 further down the coast in Los Angeles. His sound was well known and he had featured on Don McLean's classic Buddy Holly inspired 'American Pie', a huge hit in 1973. His association with Bob Dylan was to last for the Rolling Thunder Review and the 1978 tour of the Far East that resulted in the 'Live At Budokan' album released the following year. He has also played with Bruce Springsteen and Billy Idol among others.

Bobby Neuwirth had first met Dylan back in the folk days of the early sixties in Massachusetts and they had subsequently built a lasting friendship. Neuwirth is also a poet, singer, songwriter and respected record producer. His main claim to fame up until that point had been the track 'Mercedes Benz' that he had co written with the late Janis Joplin, who had also been managed by Albert Grossman before her tragically premature death in October 1970.

The early backbone of what would become the Rolling Thunder Revue was taking shape. Another significant event occurred in late June 1975 when, legend has it, Dylan was driving through the streets around The Village when he spotted an attractive girl with long hair, carrying a violin case, walking along the sidewalk. Her name was Scarlet Rivera and she couldn't quite believe it when he asked her back to his studio to run through some of his new songs.

Her arrival was of almost mystical timing, as she would go on to produce the haunting violin sound that made 'Desire' such a wonderfully blended album. Her work with Dylan included her famous appearance on the World Of John Hammond television special, and she also appeared in the 'Renaldo and Clara' film. Since then Scarlet has gone on to become a solo artist in her own right producing many wonderfully atmospheric moments. Back in 1975, however, she was largely unknown, and her sudden elevation to playing on live television with Bob Dylan was a dream beyond her wildest dreams.

Once in the studio, Dylan ran her through his new work 'Isis', 'Mozambique' and 'One More Cup Of Coffee' and the magical blend that would soak through 'Desire' was created. Soon after he took Scarlet to see Muddy Waters (d. 1983) at one of Dylan's favourite haunts, The Bottom Line Club, New York where they ended up jamming with the jazz legend. He also appeared up on stage with Ramblin' Jack Elliott at The

Other End, another well-frequented club in The Village, and was backed by Rob Stoner on bass. Bobby Neuwirth was there, also.

It was Neuwirth who invited Steven Soles along to meet Dylan. They had briefly met back in 1968, and West Coast-based Soles was no doubt unaware that he was being auditioned, in a loose sense, and it would result in his participation on Rolling Thunder. Soles also appeared on 'Street Legal' in 1978 and also formed 'The Alpha Band' along with soon to be Rolling Thunder players T-Bone Burnett and David Mansfield. He has released several solo albums and has also produced Peter Case, Elvis Costello, Roy Orbison, Don McLean and Rolling Thunder's Roger McGuinn. When Neuwirth's ad hoc band appeared at The Other End on a weeklong booking, they were seen by Mick Ronson and Ian Hunter, both from the United Kingdom.

It wouldn't take long for Ronson to join them on stage and take on lead guitar. Mick Ronson, who sadly died aged 46 in 1993, had made a name for himself playing with David Bowie on albums such as 'The Man Who Sold The World', 'Hunky Dory', 'Aladdin Sane', 'Rise and Fall of Ziggy Stardust and 'The Spiders From Mars'. He had also worked with New York's Lou Reed and had produced his 'Transformer' album. In 1973 he parted company with Bowie and had teamed up with Ian Hunter in Mott The Hoople. His association with Hunter would go on to produce many classic tracks. He also worked with Morrissey, Elton John, John Mellencamp and appeared at the Freddie Mercury Memorial Concert 1992.

By getting up on stage with Neuwirth's collection of musicians he all but secured his place on The Rolling Thunder Revue. Perhaps significantly, in the light of Dylan's subsequent religious conversion, Ronson was, at that time, an active member of The Church of the Latter Day Saints.

Next to become involved was seventeen-year-old David Mansfield, who was invited up on to the stage by Neuwirth along with Texan based T- Bone Burnett. Mansfield had achieved a reputation as being a more than competent violin and mandolin player and, despite his first band being called rather bizarrely 'Quacky Duck and His Barnyard Friends', was approached by Dylan soon after arriving in New York to join the Rolling Thunder. After it ended, he joined forces with Soles and Burnett in The Alpha Band, carrying on where the Thunder Revue had ended, releasing three albums 'The Alpha Band', 'Spark In The Dark' (both in 1977), and finally 'Statue Makers Of Hollywood' the following year. In 1980 he wrote the score for the film 'Heaven's Gate' and appeared in a small cameo role. Later, he was part of The Range band who backed Bruce Hornsby playing mandolin on 'Mandolin Rain' in 1986.

BOB DYLAN FREEWHEELIN HIS LIFE AND MUSIC

T-Bone Burnett was nearly twenty years the senior of Mansfield having been born Joseph Henry Burnett in St Louis in 1948. He had been raised in Texas and first came to prominence in 1972 with his first album 'The B52 Band and The Fabulous Skylarks'. After leaving The Alpha Band in 1978, he has since won a Grammy for his work on the film 'Oh Brother Where Art Thou?' and was an Oscar nominee for his score for the film 'Cold Mountain'. He has worked with Tony Bennett, the late Warren Zevon, Elvis Costello, Emmylou Harris, Arlo Guthrie, Roy Orbison and K.D. Lang. He also worked with Joaquin Phoenix and Reese Witherspoon for the portrayal of Johnny and June Carter Cash in the film 'Walk The Line'.

The Rolling Thunder group of musicians was taking shape as Dylan continued work on what was to become the 'Desire' album. For this, he teamed up with stage director Jacques Levy (died 2004). New York-based Levy first appeared in theatre circles in 1965, when he directed Sam Shepard's 'Red Cross' play. His other work included Jean-Claude van Italy's 'America Hurrah' and more famously the 1969 Broadway production of the controversial but acclaimed 'Oh! Calcutta!'. As a result of his involvement with this he had met The Byrds' founder member Roger McGuinn, and through him had been introduced to Bob Dylan.

Levy would co-write seven songs on 'Desire' with Dylan over a three-week period of retreat, namely 'Isis', 'Mozambique', 'Oh Sister', 'Romance In Durango', 'Black Diamond Bay', and bring his more disciplined stage approach to 'Joey' and 'Hurricane'. It was Levy who had kicked off the opening lines of 'Hurricane', helping to make it read like a script or a screenplay and setting the scene for the song perfectly. 'Pistol shots ring out in a bar room night' and 'This is the story of the Hurricane'. His collaboration on the album cannot be understated, and he brought a discipline and structure to Dylan's ideas that fully enhanced the songs, making 'Desire' one of his best ever albums. Had 'Desire' not followed the masterful 'Blood On The Tracks' it would no doubt be a contender for his best album ever, such was the strength of material and musicianship contained within. Either way he had achieved the near impossible and followed such an album with one as strong as anything he had previously produced.

Appearing on the album were Rob Stoner, Howard Wyeth and Scarlet Rivera, soon to be Rolling Thunder personnel. Emmylou Harris, who had previously worked with the recently departed Gram Parsons (died 1973), also appears and provides background vocals. Harris has since become one of the leading lights in her genre, performing with all the very best, such as Neil Young, Willie Nelson, Dolly Parton and Linda Ronstadt.

BOB DYLAN FREEWHEELIN HIS LIFE AND MUSIC

The first track to be recorded was 'Joey', on July 14th 1975. This was inspired through his reading of the Donald Goddard book on New York gangster Joey Gallo. In fact, both Levy and Dylan had recently attended a dinner given by members of Gallo's family. Joey, who had died three years earlier in 1972, was a gunman and racketeer for the Profaci family, later the Colombo family, who had been born into a Brooklyn teeming with crime and violent criminals. He quickly gained a reputation as a willing gunman and assassin. In the 1940's and 50's, he and his two brothers attempted to take control of powerful mafia family the Profaci's. He was convicted of extortion in 1961 and served ten years in jail before reappearing in 1971.

Profaci's successor was Joe Colombo, and on his release Gallo rose again to challenge his new rival. In June 1971, Colombo was fatally shot by Jerome Johnson, who in turn was shot dead by bodyguards before he could flee the scene. Johnson's association with Gallo shifted attention to him, and on April 7th 1972, whilst out with his family celebrating his 43rd birthday in Umberto's Clam Bar in Mulberry Street in the area known as Little Italy in New York, he was gunned down and died out in the street trying to draw the shots away from his family.

It was a New York story through and through, and although sounding like something from the 1930's, was, in fact, clear in the recent memory of the city's citizens, including of course Bob Dylan. The song was controversial and was criticised for the apparent glorification of a man who had been a killer in his time.

The session to record this track included The Dave Mason Band, a five-piece outfit that included three female backing singers along with mandolin, violin and accordion. The result did not make the cut, and a track about Rita Mae Brown was also discarded. The band did not appear when sessions were revisited exactly two weeks later on July 28th.

Dave Mason had been born in Worcester, England and was a close friend of Jimi Hendrix, who had died in September 1970. It was at a party that both attended that Mason had played Bob Dylan's 'All Along The Watchtower' to Hendrix, and the American guitarist adopted it, recording it with Mason on acoustic guitar. Dave Mason had been a member of the band Traffic, and went on to play with the likes of George Harrison (d. 2001), Eric Clapton and Cass Elliott (d. 1974). In the eighties, he briefly joined Fleetwood Mac before resuming a solo career that continues to this day.

Once Dylan had decided not to invite the Mason Band back, he assembled another group of more than twenty musicians for the second 'Desire' sessions. Included in this massive gathering was guitar legend Eric Clapton of Cream and Yardbirds fame. Guitarist Neil Hubbard also joined in the sessions, which seems an odd move as Dylan already had Clapton on board. Hubbard had been playing as part of Joe Cocker's Grease Band back in the early seventies.

It did not take long to see that the big band sound that Dylan was trying to create was simply not working, and the sessions were often chaotic and disorganised. Emmylou Harris has gone on record as saying that she found Dylan's studio technique almost impossible to cope with. Six-piece English band Kokomo were also in the sessions, but only saxophonist Mel Collins and conga playing Jody Linscott were invited back, as Dylan tried to find the right mix that he could clearly hear in his mind. Collins has subsequently become one of the most in-demand saxophone session players, and has appeared on albums with the likes of Eric Clapton. King Crimson, Roger Waters, Pete Townshend, The Rolling Stones, Dire Straits, Bad Company, Uriah Heep and many others in an amazingly successful career.

Hugh McCracken and guitarist Vinnie Bell were also present. McCracken has become another extremely accomplished session musician, playing with The Grateful Dead, James Taylor, Jefferson Airplane, Carly Simon, Paul Simon, Billy Joel and all four solo performing Beatles. A New Yorker, he was born in 1935, and played with all the greats of the New York scene throughout the sixties. He also worked with Tony Mottola, Frankie Valli, Dionne Warwick, Frank Sinatra and even The Monkees. Fellow New Yorker Dom Cortese covered the accordion. Born way back in 1921 Cortese has played with Elvis Presley and Billy Joel before his death in 2001. Luther Rix sat in and covered percussion.

With the sessions falling apart in confusion, producer Don Devito finally approached Rob Stoner for advice, and as a result, a more trimmed-down gathering reconvened for the subsequent sessions. A drummer was required, and Stoner suggested that his colleague Howie Wyeth be tried out. Wyeth, who moved into New York City in 1968, was extremely popular both as a musician and a person. He went on to play on both this and the 'Hard Rain' live album, having toured with the Rolling Thunder Revue and again on the 1978 tour. He returned to work in New York, and he could play jazz, rockabilly and many other styles, switching between them whilst always giving his all. In March 1996, his life came to a premature end when, at the age of 51, Wyeth died of a heart attack in the city's St Vincent Hospital.

The trimmed-down version went well, and pretty soon most of the album had been recorded, during a mammoth session lasting until eight the next morning. Of the songs they recorded that night, only 'Rita Mae' didn't make it onto the album. A final session was called on the 31st, and this time, Sara Dylan was present to hear her husband record the

track 'Sara' that he wrote for her, along with 'Romance In Durango' and a track called 'Abandoned Love'.

The album itself is a triumph, particularly when you consider the chaotic environment it was created in. But, once again, Dylan had managed to get the whole thing evolving and peaking at exactly the right moment to, somehow, come up with an album of supreme quality. Starting with the epic 'Hurricane', he introduces the sound of Scarlet Rivera to us and opens with all the confidence of a truly masterful songwriter with this gigantic performance. 'Isis' follows, and is a mystical swirl of visions that once again has Rivera providing even more colour to an already rich work. 'Isis' is a travelogue contained within a massive scope, as it moves from scene to scene in a now typically poetic story-telling style. A mystical journey, it ignites and inspires the imagination as only Dylan can.

'Mozambique' is another Dylan/Levy combination, and moves the album on in an atmospheric mood where 'Isis' left off. Containing every possible word ending that rhymes with the title, it shows the strength and enjoyment within the partnership with Levy. Altogether lighter, it still conjures powerful imagery and includes some wonderful backing vocals. Once again, Rivera's sweeping violin provides the background to a superbly crafted song. This is the case for the haunting 'One More Cup Of Coffee', another stunningly evocative track and a jewel even in this strong set. Once again, the backing vocals underpin Dylan's voice, and the stripped-down backing works so well, it is hard to imagine the track in any other way.

Ms. Blakley was, at the time of the album, busy working on the film 'Nashville', playing country great Barbara Jean, and her acting career would continue with an appearance in 'Renaldo & Clara'.

'Oh Sister' follows on magically and lyrically and would soon become a regular part of the live set. 'Joey' arrives and delivers a twelve-verse rendition of Dylan's controversial take on Joey Gallo, who had only recently been killed. Feelings were obviously still running high at the time and the track resulted in several scathing reviews for its content. 'Romance in Durango' was the only track that came from the big band sound that Dylan had envisaged for the album. The track is essentially a story of an outlaw escaping through Mexico and is a reminder of Dylan's Alias persona in Sam Peckinpah's film: 'Pat Garrett and Billy The Kid'.

'Black Diamond Bay' is a disturbing song delivered in an upbeat tempo about death and destruction during an earthquake on a small island. Seen through different eyes, it tells of how the different people reacted to the realisation that death awaited. The final track, 'Sara', is perhaps Dylan's most direct confirmation of the love of his life and was recorded in her presence at a time when they were busy trying to repair their marriage. It visits scenes throughout their time together and is as perfect a dedication of undying love as any songwriter is likely to produce.

Dylan had pulled the album back from the brink and managed to create a collection of songs as strong as anything he had attempted before. Once it was complete, he went on a short vacation with Sara and the family to their farm in Minnesota before travelling out to Chicago to appear on a televised recognition of the life of John Hammond the record producer and music critic who died in 1987. There had been very little warning and very little time to practice, but once again he pulled it out of the hat and guided a visibly nervous Scarlet Rivera through a superb set that included a powerful version of 'Hurricane'.

'Hurricane' had caused some legal controversy, and a line regarding Bello and Bradley had to be removed before it was aired on television to prevent litigation. The decision was made to re-record the whole track prior to release to eliminate the offending line. For this, Ronee Blakley stood in on background vocals and Luther Rix on drums. It was felt by those present that the re-recorded version lacked something of the original spark, but as a listener it is impossible to tell.

'Desire' was finally released to an eager audience early in 1976, and it was well received by a public who had doubted whether Dylan could maintain the style that had been 'Blood On The Tracks'. Meanwhile, he had been busy gathering even more musicians for his Rolling Thunder adventure. He wanted it to take the form of a travelling circus, turning up almost unannounced at smaller more, intimate venues, with Dylan and his troupe of diverse musicians putting on a mammoth show lasting upwards of four hours.

The Rolling Thunder Revue would, once again, break new ground with each night being different from anything that had gone before, and even the musicians not being entirely sure what would happen next. It would be during the Revue that the now familiar trademark would evolve of Dylan meshing his songs into one another, changing tempo, key and arrangement in an attempt to keep it fresh and exciting; like a live circus keeping both audience and band on their edge of their seats. Quite often, he would announce one song and suddenly launch into something else. Even musicians of the quality of Mick Ronson, Joan Baez and Roger McGuinn had to continuously watch the man himself to see where they were heading. It was a livewire act to music, and what Dylan wanted most, not for the first time, was to take away the comfort and predictability of a safety net.

CHAPTER THREE

Joining the band that already consisted of Dylan, Rob Stoner, Ramblin' Jack Elliott, Howie Wyeth, T-Bone Burnett, Scarlet Rivera, Steven Soles, David Mansfield, Bob Neuwirth and Mick Ronson, would be Joan Baez, Roger McGuinn, Kinky Friedman, Ronee Blakley, Allen Ginsberg and Joni Mitchell. Joan Baez had been a large part of the early Dylan's life both professionally and privately before he had turned his back on the folk music she performed so magnificently and turned electric. Born Joan Chandos Baez to a Quaker family in New York State just a few months before Bob Dylan, she developed an early interest in politics when her father, a physicist of some renown, apparently refused to help his Government with a project to build an atomic bomb during the height of the Cold War.

This resulted in her lifelong interest in political activism. Her family moved around the globe, living temporarily in France, Italy, Switzerland and, most significantly, Iraq when she was ten years old, where she witnessed first hand the effects of extreme poverty. At the age of fifteen she saw Martin Luther King Jnr. deliver a speech, which had a profound effect. She was greatly influenced by his message of a non-violent response to civil rights and racism.

The following year Joan bought her first guitar and began to learn to play. Her outspoken political views resulted in her being labelled a communist sympathiser at school during a time when political paranoia was sweeping the States as the Cold War took hold. In 1958, the Baez family moved to Belmont, near Boston, a town that was the centre of a thriving folk music scene. It was here that she started to perform at the local clubs and bars, and soon after she made her first recording.

It was a rather modest effort called 'Folksingers 'Round Harvard Square', now a collector's dream. The following year she was invited by Bob Gibson to perform at the Newport Folk Festival, and her appearance caused quite a stir, resulting in a contract with Vanguard Records.

Her first Vanguard album was recorded in 1960 and contained folk standards and blues covers. It wasn't until her second album (Joan Baez Volume 2) that sales really took off. This and her next few albums all went gold, and suddenly she found herself among the elite of the American Roots Revival.

In 1962, a young Bob Dylan arrived on the scene and the two began a romance that would last until the mid sixties. One of her best-known songs of the period was written by Dylan: 'Love Is Just a Four Letter Word', a song that the writer himself never recorded. After splitting with Dylan she met and married David Harris, a prominent anti-Vietnam war activist. In July 1969, just a year after their marriage, and while Joan was pregnant, Harris was arrested and imprisoned for fifteen months having refused his draft. Baez's appearance at the Woodstock Festival in 1969 secured her a status worldwide.

In 1973 the couple were divorced and she has never re-married. Baez's recording career has continued strongly, switching to A & M Records in 1972, and she re-united with Dylan on stage for the Rolling Thunder Revue. This coincided with her biggest-selling album to date, 'Diamonds & Rust', the title song being about her relationship with Dylan.

Throughout her career she has remained loyal to her political ideals, which have always been at the forefront of her work. In 1967 she was twice arrested during protests against the Vietnam War, and in 1972 she travelled to North Vietnam along with a peace delegation. In the early seventies Joan was involved in forming a United States branch of Amnesty International. Then, in 1979, she took a four-page advert in four leading American newspapers to publish her views on the Communist Government in Vietnam. This put her at odds with other prominent leading activists of the time such as actress Jane Fonda.

As a result of, this Baez formed her own human rights group, Humanitas International, and she toured South America in response to reported oppression and civil rights abuses. She has campaigned on behalf of gay and lesbian issues, has been lifted by crane with environmentalists to sit in trees when they were threatened, protested against the U.S. invasion of Iraq and performed with Steve Earle and Emmylou Harris to raise awareness of landmines. Even now, in her mid-seventies, she continues to be both musically and politically active, and recently took part in another tree sit in Los Angeles.

The relationship with Bob Dylan began when the two met in Greenwich Village in 1961. Baez was already a recording artist and Dylan was unknown. In 1963, they shared a stage together, and his early protest

songs struck a chord with her own political views. However, by the time of his tour of Europe in 1965, he had moved away from his folk roots and controversially gone electric. He had also met his future wife Sara, effectively ending his relationship with Joan. She has written several songs about her love for Dylan, namely 'Diamonds and Rust', which she would perform during solo slots on the Rolling Thunder Revue, 'To Bobby' (1972), 'Winds Of The Old Days' (1975), 'Time Is Passing Us By' and 'O Brother' (both 1976). When their relationship ended amongst the storm of Dylan's new love for Sara, there were inevitably bad feelings between them. However, on stage together for The Rolling Thunder Revue, the closeness and chemistry between them is almost tangible.

Another high-profile addition was long-term friend and admirer Roger McGuinn. Born a year after Dylan in 1942 in Chicago as James Joseph McGuinn III, he had first come to prominence in the early sixties as Jim McGuinn, part of the Chad Mitchell Trio, a band that would later feature John Denver (d. 1997) among it's members, before being employed briefly as a backing guitarist to chart-topping Bobby Darin (d. 1973) and Judy Collins.

The Beatles' explosion had a profound effect on the young McGuinn, and by July 1964, inspired by what he heard, he and Gene Clark (d.1991) formed 'The Byrds'.

'The Byrds' adopted a Beatlesque look, but their sound was flowered by McGuinn's distinctive, ringing 'jingle jangle' twelve string Rickenbacker guitar. He was also one of the first western musicians to experiment on the Sitar, and it's distinctive sound can be heard on their 1966 classic, 'Eight Miles High'. He also appeared with a seven string guitar featuring a double G- string, the second of which was tuned an octave higher.

At the height of their success, 'The Byrds' lineup featured McGuinn, Clark, David Crosby (later of Crosby, Stills Nash and Young), Chris Hillman and drummer Michael Clark (d. 1993), but would go on to include Gram Parsons (d. 1973), Gene Parsons and Clarence White (d. 1973). They had their first successes in 1965 with a cover of Bob Dylan's 'Mr. Tambourine Man', and followed that with the Biblically based 'Turn, Turn, Turn'.

In 1965, Jim McGuinn became Roger when he was initiated into the Subud religion. Subud is an international spiritual group for people of all religious beliefs, and practices meditation to connect with God, or the Great Life Force. During one of these sessions, McGuinn reportedly received guidance that the letter 'R' would be of relevance for him, and he offered several names beginning with 'R' to his Guru. At the time, McGuinn was interested in Science Fiction, and chose names reflecting

that theme, including Ramjet, Retro and Rocket before his Guru wisely settled on Roger.

'The Byrds' evolved their folk-rock persona further, and with Gram Parsons on board finally produced a Country album with 1968's classic 'Sweethearts Of The Rodeo'. After The Byrds, Roger produced several solo albums before his old friend Bob Dylan called and asked him to join the Rolling Thunder Revue. Significantly, in the light of what was to develop in Dylan's life, McGuinn became a born again Christian in 1977.

Kinky Friedman was known for his alternative satirist approach to music when he became involved with Rolling Thunder. Originating from Texas, his first band, the bizarrely named 'King Arthur and The Carrots', ridiculed surf music; his next band was called 'Kinky Friedman and The Texas Jewboys'. Branching out on his own, he had, by 1973, achieved a reputation as a country and western solo performer and attracted huge controversy with his 'They Ain't Makin' Jews Like Jesus Anymore', and his most famous song 'Asshole From El Paso'.

Dylan greatly admired Patti Smith and often saw her perform in Greenwich Village. He approached her but she declined to join him. However, in her stead another prominent female performer, Joni Mitchell, subsequently joined, albeit temporarily. Canadian Mitchell, who shunned the music industry in 2007 preferring to devote her time to art (her first love) that she exhibits but does not sell, had been born Roberta Joan Anderson in 1943. She had come to notice as a folk singer, having taken the name Mitchell from a brief marriage to fellow folkie Chuck Mitchell, and was famed for her extraordinary vocal range and alternative guitar tunings. The Byrds' David Crosby first noticed her whilst she was playing 'The Gaslight South Club' in Florida. He encouraged her to move to the west coast, and she quickly settled in Los Angeles. Her reputation as a songwriter attracted attention, and her songs were covered by the likes of George Hamilton IV, who released 'Urge For Going', and Judy Collins who covered 'Both Sides Now'.

Even across the Atlantic in Britain her songs were being noticed and admired, with 'Fairport Convention' releasing a Mitchell-written song 'Chelsea Morning' in 1967. Her most famous song was perhaps 'Woodstock', and fully captured the mood of a generation. It was successfully covered by Crosby, Stills and Nash and also made a hit by 'Matthews Southern Comfort'. Sadly she wrote it after the event, having missed performing there due to a television commitment, a management decision that has saddened her ever since. Perhaps her best-known record, and the one that made her a household name was 'Big Yellow Taxi'. In 1971 she released an album in many ways similar in mood to Dylan's later 'Blood On The Tracks'. 'Blue' is a confessional album that explored the many highs and lows of relationships. By the time she walked in on the Rolling Thunder Revue, she was a world acclaimed performer and had just released her most diverse work up until that point with her 1975 album 'The Hissing Of The Summer Lawns'. Subsequently she moved into a more jazz-inspired style and continued to release successful albums before working alongside artists like Don Henley, Billy Idol, Tom Petty, Willie Nelson, and Roger Waters for his massive representation of 'The Wall' in Berlin. In 1994, her album 'Turbulent Indigo' won her a long overdue Grammy and was seen as a return to a more accessible style. In 1998 she once again toured with Bob Dylan whilst promoting her album 'Tiger'.

Sitting just on the periphery of the Revue was David Blue. A one-time partner of Joni Mitchell and a friend of Dylan's dating way back to the early Village days, he had included Ronee Blakely in his band when Dylan had called in to see him perform. Blakely would join the Revue as a backing singer, having appeared on the 'Desire' album. Blue, whose real name is Stuart David Cohen, arrived in Greenwich Village and worked as a dishwasher in The Gaslight Café, where Allen Ginsberg would perform readings and Jack Elliott would sing. Inevitably, being part of that scene at that time meant a meeting with Dylan, and in early 1963 they crossed paths. Dylan encouraged his new songwriting friend to perform, and he adopted the name Blue following a suggestion from Eric Anderson. He contacted Dylan to find out the procedure for changing a name, only to have him singing 'It's All Over Now David Blue' at him.

Their friendship grew and remained solid throughout the remainder of Blue's life. In 1966, Blue released an album of his own Dylan-inspired work before forming his own band 'The American Patrol', releasing the acclaimed 1968 album 'These 23 Days In September'.

By the time of the Revue, Blue needed a break. His marriage to another Sara and the subsequent traumatic breakdown resulted in the often sadly haunting albums 'Me' in 1970, and 'Stories' two years later. His next album was produced by another friend Graham Nash and won accolades as being frighteningly honest and introspective. Despite all of this he remained in the shadow of Dylan and other contemporaries, and is remembered as much for his brief acting career. He appeared in 'Renaldo and Clara' and received good reviews for several other films.

When he returned to New York in the seventies, he continued his dual career and wrote a song called 'Children Of Rock and Roll' that recounted a generation that had lost so many souls along the journey. Sadly, Blue would soon follow when, in 1982, he died from a massive heart attack whilst out in Washington Square Park aged only forty-one.

His death hit Dylan hard.

The first concert on The Rolling Thunder Revue was scheduled for Plymouth, Massachusetts. In a reaction to the near hysteria that he had experienced on tour the previous year, Dylan had created a concept unlike anything that had been tried before. It would not be a Bob Dylan show, but would include all the other musicians in a rolling and unpredictable format. The fact that the whole concept had been worked on with Jacques Levy illustrates the theatrical slant. Great thought had been given by Levy about the best way to introduce Dylan to the stage, and Levy almost choreographically planned Dylan's entry. Of course, Dylan would change the sequence around, and the Revue became exactly what he had first envisaged, developing it's own life force as it moved from town to town.

Allen Ginsberg joined the troupe as Revue Poet, and during several rehearsals at a nearby Plymouth Hotel, plans began to take shape that would reflect the whole carnival atmosphere of the idea. It would travel from venue to venue, each of them chosen initially for their more intimate and smaller capacities than Dylan had experienced on his stadium-sized tour the previous year. It would be Joan Baez's first appearance in public with him for ten years. It would feature a whole range of musicians and influences, including 'names' like McGuinn, Baez, Ronson and Elliott and the not so well known like Neuwirth and Stoner, to the unknown talents of young David Mansfield.

It would be this tour that gave Dylan the opportunity to almost reinvent himself on a nightly basis, a skill he has employed and enjoyed right through his 'Never Ending Tour' and up to today. He would come on and play the set fast one night or slow it down for the next. He would change key unannounced, switch set lists, stop and start songs and introduce whole new starts to even his best-known songs so that the band wouldn't realise what they were playing until the vocals kicked in. In essence it sounded like a recipe for disaster, but we are talking about one of, if not, the greatest performers of all time and the results were often spectacular in their unpredictability.

Rob Stoner describes, in Clinton Heylin's 'Behind The Shades', of how 'Isis' would be played in reggae, or funk or even waltz. In the same book Mick Ronson describes how he constantly had to get into a position where he could actually see Dylan's guitar to know what chord the band were moving into. The resulting sound is fresh, exciting and highly original. It is also some of Dylan's finest live music. It was a situation that would have fazed many a musician, but the band stayed loyal to the concept, maybe accepting that it was a price worth paying to be on stage with Bob Dylan.

One third of the whole set would have Dylan taking centre stage with more than half of the material being gleaned from 'Desire'. Regular appearances included 'Isis' and 'Romance in Durango', during which, Scarlet Rivera would add her extraordinarily colourful violin. Other tracks to feature strongly would be 'Hurricane', 'Oh Sister', 'One More Cup Of Coffee', 'Sara', 'Knockin' On Heavens Door', 'Simple Twist Of Fate', 'Mozambique', 'Tangled Up In Blue', 'Just Like A Woman' and even Woody Guthrie's 'This Land Is Your Land'. Dylan would also share the stage with Bobby Neuwirth, a spot that had them both blasting out 'When I Paint My Masterpiece' with an often bemused looking Neuwirth apparently trying to double guess what version, timing, key or style Dylan would be using on that particular night. His set shared with Joan Baez would revolve through renditions of some of his earlier days, such as 'I Pity The Poor Immigrant' or 'Deportee' and once again he would tease and taunt her by changing things around unannounced, or even launching into an unrehearsed song from a long time before.

There was an undeniable circus atmosphere to the whole event. It would have been totally possible to have seen every one of the thirty shows throughout the autumn of that year and never be able to fully predict what would be heard. The band was clearly on the edge of a chasm of uncertainty but it was a situation that they seemed to revel in, and without doubt that extra level of concentration required to keep up with Dylan resulted in some astonishing performances.

The circus atmosphere was further underlined by Dylan's decision to sometimes wear make up. Perhaps inspired by the whole festival feel to the occasion, or due to Mick Ronson's influence from his time with Bowie, he typically only wore it on some nights, again without any sense of predictability. He would paint his face into an almost ghost like appearance, similar to that of the great mime artists. He took it one step further by appearing in a plastic face-mask before it had to come off to enable him to play the mouth organ.

In later interviews, Dylan explained that he saw it more of a representation of the 'Commedia Dell'Arte' who, fittingly, were a troupe of performers who travelled primarily around Italy, each player adopting masks or make up to represent their individual role in life and within the production, and performed a purely visual representation without script, improvising their characters as the performer felt that they should. This perfectly explains where Dylan was coming from within the Rolling Thunder Revue concept.

This freedom of expression was enjoyed by the musicians involved, as each was given every opportunity to express themselves freely every night and a chance to take the music off in different directions. It appealed to every ounce of the myriad of creativity contained within the band and resulted in some magical performances. Joan Baez even adopted the make up occasionally as the improvisational concept was fully realised.

Clinton Heylin's book has Steven Soles describing the experience as exciting and as an adrenalin rush within the freedom of the expression of an idea. Filmmakers Larry Johnson and Mel Howard were brought in to film the Revue, alongside Sam Shepard, and the resulting footage provides a fascinating insight that could have almost endless consequences. The footage shot would also form scenes for the 'Renaldo and Clara' project with Sara Dylan; Joan Baez and extended cast making appearances. Shepard saw himself primarily as a scriptwriter for 'Renaldo and Clara', but soon realised that there was little space for him due to its ambiguous and improvisational form. Shepard of course has subsequently gone on to achieve many successes of note as a writer, actor, producer and playwright. It was his screenplay that made 'Paris Texas' such a cult film.

The improvisational basis resulted in many miles of footage that have never been officially seen. Joan Baez, by her own admission, found being exposed to the camera an uncomfortable experience but tried valiantly to make her appearances fulfill their aim. Joni Mitchell, however, later withdrew her permission for her scenes to be included. Of course, one of the main players on set was Dylan's wife Sara, and the combination of all the women together, including Ronee Blakely, produced some difficult moments. Joni Mitchell joined the tour half way through, merely intending to visit to see what was happening but ended up staying at her own expense and put in several performances.

Attracted by the camaraderie and enthusiasm for the whole project, she stayed long enough to write lyrics illustrating her rather low view of Blakely in her song 'Shades Of Scarlet Conquering'. Blakely, maybe sensing the tension between the various combinations of herself, Baez, Mitchell and of course Sara, who made it known that she did not trust her with her husband, left the Revue. Some tension was relieved when Joan Baez dressed as Bob Dylan and went out on stage, causing great confusion among the audience in the process.

On stage, the Baez and Dylan combination resulted in some tender and humorous moments. She was seen to playfully kick him from behind and he would tease and taunt her by suddenly, temporarily pausing a song and tricking her into singing in the gap.

Dylan, meanwhile, was spending most of his time when not on stage, with Howard Alk. Alk had been a major part of Dylan's life for some time. He had worked as a cameraman on both the 1965 and 1966 tours and assisted Dylan with editing both 'Eat The Document' and 'Renaldo and Clara'. His friendship and influence cannot be understated, and his suicide

CHAPTER THREE

in 1982, following a lengthy struggle with heroin, devastated Dylan. It was made worst by the fact that it occurred at The Rundown, a studio that Dylan had set up, and felt quite comfortable with.

Alk had, several days before his death, even turned down an invitation to be presented with an award, passing on his apologies by saying that he would not be able to attend as he would be busy committing suicide that night. It was a fitting comment from one of the people who had travelled the distance in amongst the mania of his time with Bob Dylan.

Inevitably, as word of the Revue spread, the demand for tickets was such that larger venues were chosen. It was not a development that Dylan wanted to happen, but the situation forced a need to adjust a financial loss brought about by the logistics of moving such a large travelling circus from small place to small place. Several larger events were booked, namely in Providence, New Haven, Maple Leaf Gardens in Toronto and Montreal's Forum. Much of the performance at The Forum was captured on film, and shows the band at the very top of their game during what was an ever-shifting journey. They also appeared at a huge benefit show for Hurricane Carter that was arranged for December the 8th 1975 at New York's Madison Square Garden. The show ran it's full four hours, and the media reviews were ecstatic.

In amongst all of this furore, 1976 arrived with 'Desire' finally released. In retrospect, it is hard to imagine the Revue performing a lot of the 'Desire' material without it first being supported by the album. It proved a great success and provided Dylan with the third album of his career to top the charts on both sides of the Atlantic. Its release coincided with the final, often tempestuous, days of the Dylan marriage. As he began rehearsals to take the Revue back on tour, two events would change the direction of his life.

Firstly he met and began a relationship with actress Sally Kirkland. The Goddaughter of the late Shelley Winters was part of the Andy Warhol scene in New York in the seventies, becoming the first actress to appear nude on stage when she starred in the 1968 production of 'Sweet Eros'. She can also be seen, not quite so revealingly, in 'The Sting', 'The Way We Were', 'A Star Is Born' and 'Private Benjamin', all major blockbusters of their day. In 1987 she was nominated for a best actress award for her part in 'Anna'.

Despite her obvious attractiveness, it was also her free-spirited nature that drew Dylan's eye. She became a Minister in the Church of the Movement of Spiritual Awareness teaching drama, yoga and meditation. Later, she also hosted a show on the syndicated HealthyLife Radio Network and still continues her acting career. Unbeknown to all

but those closest to him, Dylan was about to embark on a journey of spiritual enlightenment of his own.

The second event that would change Dylan's outlook occurred on April the 9th 1973 when Phil Ochs was found hanged in his sister's New York apartment. Dylan, who was out having dinner with the band when told of the death of Ochs, reacted with both sadness and anger at the news. The relationship had been a difficult one throughout its last years because Ochs' mental state had deteriorated to the point where he had become delusional and often threatening. All the same, it was a visibly shocked Dylan that reflected on whether the situation could have been changed had Ochs been involved in the tour; a situation that was, without doubt, impossible following the incident that occurred when they had last met when Ochs' paranoia turned against him.

When the second Revue tour finally kicked off with dates on the Golf Coast, some of the spontaneity and freshness was understandably missing. The continuing drama of his increasingly unpleasant break-up from Sara and the news of the suicide of an old friend resulted in him being withdrawn and hard to communicate with. He expressed some of this tension by bringing a rougher, more electric sound to his guitar, and despite the continued presence of some quality guitarists, pushed his own sometimes-erratic National guitar, which was heavy on distortion, out to the front.

As the marriage entered its final death throes, he performed more tracks from 'Blood On The Tracks', often delivering the songs with an almost tangible anger. As the tour started he would be seen with any one of a number of female members of the entourage as the apparent void left by Sara's on off presence took hold once again. By the time the band arrived at Clearwater in Florida, some of the old atmosphere had returned, and a calmer Dylan emerged to deliver some telling performances.

A further complication arose when he started a relationship with Stephanie Buffington. He had told his new lady that he had officially separated from Sara some months before, but Sara suddenly re-appeared and an ugly confrontation resulted. The tour was destined not to have the demand that the first one had enjoyed and poor ticket sales following some indifferent reviews resulted in several shows being cancelled.

By the time it was due to play at Dallas and Houston, slow sales meant that the scheduled second nights were cancelled, despite Willie Nelson being invited along. The concert at San Antonio was moved from the Hemisfair Arena to the smaller, more modest location of The Municipal Auditorium. Two scheduled shows at the music capital of Austin were combined into one. All of this proved to be a major disappointment to Dylan and the Revue, following the massive successes of 'Blood On The Tracks' and 'Desire' and the demand for tickets during the first tour.

Sara's endurance finally gave way at Houston when she walked out on her husband, and maybe it was this event that led to him performing 'One Of Us Must Know', a song written about a relationship gone astray. With a sense of inevitability, he withdrew further and was reportedly drinking heavily by the time they rolled into Fort Collins. It would be the weekend that the Revue would be captured, and the subsequent album 'Hard Rain'. The album contains an edgy Dylan recorded during the continuous rain that seemed to underline his desperate mental state. The rain had come down so badly that mild shocks among the musicians occurred with frightening regularity. This was an era where several musicians had suffered similar incidents on stage, sometimes with tragic consequences.

Only a few years before, in 1972, the legendary Alex Harvey (d. 1982) lost his brother Les when he was fatally electrocuted on stage during a 'Stone The Crows' performance. Uriah Heep's Gary Thain (d.1976) had nearly suffered a similar fate, and the risk at outdoor events was such that Led Zeppelin's powerful manager Peter Grant (d. 1995) always included a 'rain no play' directive in any Zeppelin contract.

For this weekend, the rain was relentless, but in spite of all the problems the live recording still captured a moment in time when the Revue was firing on all cylinders. Of course, the recording can only be a brief moment in time as Dylan continued to keep every night different from the last.

'Hard Rain' was finally released, to include a trimmed-down set of nine tracks opening with 'Maggie's Farm', a song that still features strongly in his shows today, and moving through 'One Too Many Mornings', which had become a favourite during the Revue.

The inclusion of 'Stuck Inside Of Mobile With The Memphis Blues Again' was a surprise, dating back to the 'Blonde On Blonde' era. The album moves on with 'Oh Sister', a greatly altered 'Lay Lady Lay', 'Shelter From The Storm', 'You're A Big Girl Now', 'I Threw It All Away' and rounds off with a powerful vitriolic 'Idiot Wind'. The sound is sadly wanting in many parts of the original album, but the overall feeling of an outdoor event is captured all the same.

In places, it is superbly erratic and ramshackle as the improvisational approach comes to the fore. As a result, it acts as an important historical document of a section of Dylan's long and often diverse career. For example, the timing on the opener 'Maggie's Farm' is all over the place

as Dylan taunts and toys with it, leaving tempting gaps of different lengths as he drives the track with a performance of tantalising power. The audience reaction speaks for itself.

'One Too Many Mornings' is performed with such vocal power that it begs the question of whether he has ever been better. It is roughly produced and gloriously erratic but for any collector of Dylan this album is an absolute must as it underscores perfectly what the Rolling Thunder Revue was all about. If anything is certain with the album it is that the next night would have been different. To fully capture the tour would mean a box set of numerous discs, and who knows, one day that just may happen.

The sound on 'Stuck Inside of Mobile' reaches a new low, but again, you can almost feel the rain on the crowd and the mud under your feet. Once again, Dylan stretches the notes or cuts them short, but the band are as tight as possible in the unpredictable environment. There are times on this track when the band actually manage to dictate the pace of the song to Dylan. Complete with nerve-jangling feedback, the crowd is inevitably captured calling out for the more identifiable songs of the past.

By this time, Dylan had added drummer Gary Burke to the band. Burke has subsequently gone on to play with Joe Jackson and is currently involved in the band 'Professor Louie and the Crowmatix' who are steeped in the influence and intertwined with the history of The Band and in particular Rick Danko. The rest of the lineup is mainly drawn from the first tour, with Rob Stoner taking not only bass parts and backing vocals but also the unofficial un-elected position of band leader.

Ronson, Soles and Mansfield covered guitar, Wyeth and Burke drums, and, of course, there was Scarlet Rivera on violin. The next track is a rousing version of 'Shelter From the Storm'. Once again he pounds this out with enough passion to float it on the ample rain. It is gloriously live, un-dubbed, and every bit as real as he intended the whole Rolling Thunder party to be.

'You're A Big Girl Now' arrives next with a nicely subtle approach that features Rivera and a wonderfully acoustic pitch that sets the scene for an intimate performance that has Dylan almost appearing before you.

Yet again, he plays with each verse ending, which either works for you or doesn't, but it undoubtedly maintains every ounce of the emotion that provoked the writing of it in the first place.

It doesn't get a lot better than this and even if, like me, you are a veteran of numerous Dylan performances, it leaves you wishing you had been at this one, such is the value of the album in capturing a shot of

BOB DYLAN FREEWHEELIN HIS LIFE AND MUSIC

him at this particular liquid moment.

Scarlet Rivera had not only found her confidence by this time but beautifully added a whole brush stroke of colour to the song that makes you realise that his movement away from it subsequently, represents one of the most complete transformations or reinventions that he has made, among many, as it must have been tempting for him to further explore the possibilities that she had brought along.

'I Threw It All Away' carries on with the same degree of brilliance with Dylan once again at the height of his wave. Yet, this isn't one man and his band, and it illustrates how he had brought together a seemingly ill-fitting bunch of musicians and formed a band that grew and moved each night with a dynamism and fluidity that works on every conceivable level.

Ending with Dylan almost spitting contempt on 'Idiot Wind', the album leaves with a similar feeling as you get now when you walk out of one of his concerts having just spent an evening in the presence of genius and greatness. I don't use either expression lightly.

The last show took place at Salt Lake City and was again plagued by a strange and misguided lack of demand for tickets. Dylan knew it would be the last of what had been an incredible journey, and one that had remained loyal to its whole core, and pulled out a performance that had the smaller audience on its feet. 'Hard Rain' was aired as a television special in the September, at a time when he had turned his attention to Howard Alk and the rushes that would become 'Renaldo and Clara'. In fact, he was so wrapped up in its development that he nearly turned down Robbie Robertson's approach to appear at The Band's farewell performance, which was to be captured and immortalised in the film 'The Last Waltz'.

The film of the concert captured three glorious songs by Bob Dylan from a set of six. Backed by the legendary The Band, he started with a sublime version of 'Forever Young' that includes a superb solo from Robbie Robertson, and moved through a more ragged Rolling Thunder style version of 'Baby Let Me Follow You Down'. The finale has him being joined by the whole cast, including Van Morrison, Neil Diamond, Ringo Starr, Ron Wood, Dr. John, Joni Mitchell, Eric Clapton, Neil Young and Ronnie Hawkins for a rousing 'I Shall Be Released'. It was a fitting and moving farewell to The Band, who had, of course, been an essential part of the Dylan legacy.

In February 1977, Dylan went to Los Angeles and resumed his liaison with Sally Kirkland, but it was whilst he was busy helping Leonard Cohen with his album 'Death Of A Ladies' Man' that Sara came down to breakfast in the family house in Malibu to find her husband and children in the company of another woman, Malka. This proved to be the final act in a dying marriage and Sara released the account to a thirsty press.

Within months the divorce was finalised with Sara receiving a reported six million dollar settlement and fifty per cent of all the songs he had written during their time together. Inevitably it became messy, with tales of Dylan's alleged drug use and claims of physical violence. She also claimed that his own children had become disturbed by his 'behaviour and bizarre lifestyle' and successfully kept custody of them.

When it was finally over, Dylan moved in with the self-styled 'art healer' Farida McFree, who had been employed by Sara to help the children recover from the ordeal of the divorce. Released from the pressure of divorce and living out in Minnesota with McFree, he began work on a new set of songs that would result in his next studio album 'Street Legal'. However, he received another blow when on the 16th August 1977 he heard of the death of Elvis Presley. Dylan reacted by not speaking for days.

The recording of 'Street Legal' was shelved for nine months during which he was heavily involved in an unsuccessful attempt to gain custody of his children, who were on the verge of being moved to Hawaii, where Sara was intent on setting up a new home.

In September 1977, 'Renaldo and Clara' was finally completed and ran a total of four hours, having been edited still further from its previous length of eight, taken from over a hundred hours of footage. It had proved a massive, all-consuming task.

The influence of Norman Raeben is once again apparent in the final film, which is centred around a dream by its chief character Renaldo. Needless to say, the film, released in January 1978, received mixed reviews.

Once that was finished, work on 'Street Legal' re-commenced and for the purpose Dylan acquired a studio in Santa Monica that he named 'Rundown'. It would be Dylan's recording home for all of his studio albums up to and including 1982's 'Infidels' album.

The need to tour caught up with Dylan, and once again he asked Rob Stoner, Howie Wyeth, David Mansfield and Steven Soles to join him. Also employed, as a late replacement for Howie Wyeth (who withdrew due to a growing heroin problem), was ex-Wings drummer Denny Seiwell. To this combination he added Jesse Ed Davis (d. 1988) on guitar and as backing singers Frannie Eisenberg, Debbie Dye Gibson and Katey Sagal. When Eisenberg and Sagal left, they would be replaced by Jo Ann Harris and Helena Spring (a lifelong Christian, who would soon become romantically involved with Dylan).

'Street Legal' was finally released on June 15th 1978 with a different list of collaborators than the tour, including ex-King Crimson drummer Ian Wallace, ex-Elvis Presley TCB member Jerry Scheff on bass, Billy Cross (who would remain with Dylan for several years on lead guitar), jazzer Alan Pasqua on keys and Bobbye Hall on drums. Also involved, as backing singer, was Carolyn Dennis, who secretly became the second Mrs. Bob Dylan on the 4th June 1986. It was a marriage that, despite the birth of daughter Desiree Gabrielle Dennis-Dylan, was destined to end in divorce in October 1992.

'Street Legal' was the culmination of what had been an emotionally draining time. With the divorce, tours, and court cases 'The Last Waltz' and the negativity surrounding his 'Renaldo and Clara' film (which even included a scandalous review by 'The Village Voice' in which it wished Dylan dead), 'Street Legal' is, nonetheless, a remarkable achievement. As 'Renaldo and Clara' was being shown at the Cannes Film Festival in Southern France to mainly good reviews, Dylan released his first studio album for two years.

It was always going to be impossible to follow 'Blood On The Tracks' and 'Desire', and sure enough 'Street Legal', recorded in lightning speed over four days, falls a little short in several areas including production. Dispensing with Scarlet Rivera's violin and including a Gospel style all-girl backing group and brass gives an altogether different sound that finally has Dylan taking the big band concept into the studio.

The cryptic 'Changing Of The Guards' opens as a particular highlight. 'Baby Stop Crying', a track that was loosely based on Robert Johnson's 'Stop Breaking Down', works well within an album of songs of almost epic proportions. 'No Time To Think', for example, clocks in at a massive eight minutes. Clearly Dylan had a lot to say, and hidden in the album were many Biblical references that gave a foretaste of what was to come in his life. This was not new, as Dylan had plundered the big book on many previous occasions but clearly by this time something significant was occurring.

'Is Your Love In Vain' returns to old themes of love and the struggles of relationships, saying, 'I've been burnt before and I know the score'. Perhaps the standout track for many was the track 'Senor (Tales of Yankee Power)', which was a real show of songwriting strength from a man who had run an emotional rollercoaster for some time.

There was one more twist of fate for him during this typically turbulent time in his life and it would occur when he went back on the road with his new big band. It wouldn't be a continuation of The Rolling Thunder tours but would go on to produce not only some of the best of his live performances but also a personal event of biblical proportions.

CHAPTER THREE

BOB DYLAN FREEWHEELIN HIS LIFE AND MUSIC

Bob Dylan arrived in Japan in February 1978 to do eight shows at Budokan and a further three in Osaka. Ian Wallace replaced Danny Seiwell on the drums (Danny had been arrested during his Wings days along with Paul McCartney on a previous visit to Japan and therefore couldn't return).

From the tour, the double live album 'Budokan' (recorded during two of the dates on February 28th and March 1st) was released, highlighting an almost greatest hits approach to the material chosen. 'Budokan' contains twenty-two tracks of his best-known work, however they have, in true Dylan style, been re-arranged, giving the listener an excitement akin to hearing *"new"* material. For anyone who has never heard Dylan speak at a concert, there is the added surprise of him talking to the audience.

After 'I Shall Be Released' he becomes positively chatty, saying, *"Here's another recorded song, see if you know which one it is"*. As a double album, so much can be written, but just taking a track here and there, you have a fast and jazzy version of 'Mr. Tambourine Man'. Then there is 'Ballad Of A Thin Man', which has one of the sleaziest sax solos (performed by Steve Douglas) that I have heard in a long time.

'Don't Think Twice' has a Caribbean feel, while 'Maggie's Farm' has underlying Japanese tones. Another surprise is 'Going, Going, Gone', arranged with a slow start before suddenly bursting into a really strong rock rhythm with solo's from both the sax and guitar that are simply breathtaking.

Other tracks that stand out are a very slow version of 'Blowin' In The Wind', 'All Along The Watchtower' (which is very different from the original recording), and the classic 'Times They Are A-Changing'. In all, the album is a collection of the most recognisable songs that has Dylan performing them with typical freshness and an obvious love and respect for his Japanese audience.

Rob Stoner had been growing increasingly disenchanted with the tour, quit the band at the end of the Far East section and was replaced by Jerry Scheff. On June 13th 1978 Dylan arrived in London to play six sell-out concerts to a total audience of over one hundred thousand people at the Earls Court Arena. The European section of the tour was hailed as a great

success and confirmed his continuing iconic status on that side of the Atlantic.

'Baby Stop Crying' even gave him a top ten hit across Europe, as the tour's momentum took effect. Having enthralled audiences in Paris, Gothenburg, Rotterdam and Germany, he appeared before two hundred thousand fans at The Blackbush Airfield in Surrey. He followed this with a sixty-five-date tour of the States, and by the end of it he had given one hundred and fifteen live performances.

It was whilst on tour in Tuscon that Dylan experienced something that was to change his life totally. In his hotel room late at night he saw a powerful vision of Jesus Christ. He says in Clinton Heylin's biography: 'There was a presence in the room that couldn't have been anybody but Jesus. Jesus put his hand on me. It was a physical thing; I felt it all over me. I felt my whole body tremble. The glory of the Lord knocked me down and picked me up'.

Shortly after this experience he was seen wearing a cross during his performance at Fort Worth. For a man with a Jewish upbringing this was significant. Band members Steven Soles, T-Bone Burnett and David Mansfield were, at the time, members of the Vineyard Fellowship and invited Dylan along to build on his conversion. Declaring himself born again, Dylan embarked on writing a series of songs to form a full-on Gospel album. He brought in Dire Straits guitarist Mark Knopfler and began to work the tracks through. Knopfler had no idea, when jumping at the chance to play with Dylan, that the album would be overtly Christian. Non-believers Dire Straits drummer Pick Withers, bass player Tim Drummond and keyboardist Barry Beckett were also drafted in. The sessions would result in the 'Slow Train Coming' album, the first of a trilogy of Christian albums that included 1980's 'Saved' and 1981's 'Shot Of Love'. Despite being almost ridiculed by certain sections of the press, Dylan's born again persona attracted new fans, and suddenly his audiences would be a strange mixture of his traditional fan base eager for the classics from his colourful past and the newly added Christian followers.

His single 'Gotta Serve Somebody' taken from 'Slow Train Coming' gave him his first top thirty single in the States for over six years. The 'Slow

BOB DYLAN FREEWHEELIN HIS LIFE AND MUSIC

Train' album outsold 'Blood On The Tracks' as the curiosity for Dylan's conversion and the acceptance that it was, in fact, another quality Dylan album, solidified. It went on to remain in the album charts for six months.

His concerts became totally evangelistic in their content, with a previously detached Dylan almost preaching to his audience. The songs of old were discarded and only those reflecting his newfound love of Christ were included. He would respond to the odd walkout from the audience by taking the chance to repeat his message. There were even boos, and he had a particularly hard time when, during a six month tour, he appeared for several dates at one of his old strongholds, The Warfield, in San Francisco.

Between 'Slow Train' and 'Hanging Onto Solid Rock' he would address his audience with a full-on account of what he had learned during Bible studies at The Vineyard Fellowship. On one occasion in Arizona he was being constantly heckled by a section of the audience and launched into a lengthy and powerful rendition of 'When You Gonna Wake Up' from 'Slow Train'. Seemingly some people found it hard to reconcile the Dylan of old with this new cleaned up version. The walkouts were eagerly reported in the reviews and overshadowed the quality of the music on offer.

Taken as a trilogy the three evangelical Dylan albums are at the very least powerful and direct. The message is honestly delivered and the songs are well constructed and effective. They are all you would expect from Dylan albums except this time the message was Christian.

Standout tracks are 'When You Gonna Wake Up', 'Precious Angel', 'Gotta Serve Somebody' and 'When He Returns' from 'Slow Train', 'What Can I Do For You' on 'Saved' and 'Every Grain Of Sand' and 'Heart Of Mine' from 'Shot Of Love'. This was the album that he has gone on record as saying was his finest achievement, and the one that has given him the most pleasure and pride over the years. High stakes indeed for an album that is often overlooked in the Dylan catalogue.

When he declared his newfound faith he delivered it in typically full-on style. He rode over the sometimes cruel and sceptical reviews, he ignored the walkouts, the indifferent demand for concert tickets, the poor reviews of the albums and the constant hecklers, and in turn, he gave performances straight from the heart and a message that was taken home by more than the already saved members of his audience. He provoked thought and argument and stayed loyal to his message, ignoring demands to play his old pre-born again songs.

It wasn't the first time that he had been loudly booed and heckled, but at least no one was insensitive enough to shout 'Judas' at him this time. These three albums are often pocketed together with the assumption that he had grown tired and disillusioned with the faith by the time he released 'Infidels' in 1982.

However, if you look beneath the surface of his lyrics subsequent to the Tuscon experience his Biblical influences are never far away. Once again, he had felt that he needed to reinvent himself after three albums on the holy slow train, and that process continues up to the present day.

His albums such as the 1997 Grammy winning 'Time Out Of Mind', 2001's superb 'Love And Theft' and 2006's big-selling 'Modern Times' are some of the best material he has ever produced. On May 29th 2012, Dylan was awarded the Presidential Medal of Freedom by U.S. President Barack Obama in the White House.

Never one to follow anybody, his material continues to stand alone. Dylan's contribution to music cannot be overstated. His influence on the political world through his lyrics is without equal in music. His ability to bring injustice and prejudice to the fore is unfailing. His visionary statements truly did change the times. The term 'voice of a generation' has been used in every review of his life and will no doubt be his epitaph, despite his own denials of that role. He still maintains the ability to lead from a position outside of the arena. His catalogue of work contains immeasurable examples of the poet, the artist, the genius, the song and dance man that are the many sides of Bob Dylan. In summary, all I can say is that if his never-ending tour comes to a town near you – and throughout the 1990s and 2000s, Dylan has played almost 100 dates on the tour each year, an extraordinary schedule – it is almost criminal not to be there. There are not many chances in this world to share an hour or two in the presence of such greatness.

As Joan Baez said in her introduction to him during this Rolling Thunder Revue: 'By far the most talented crazy person that I have worked with'. Talented – unquestionably. Crazy, who can say? After all, who really knows Bob Dylan? All we do actually know as fact is the effect his music and commentary have had on our lives and surroundings. It wasn't as if Dylan was merely the right man, in the right place, at the right time, because his influence has moved far beyond that by leading a whole generation throughout a decade of immense social change. Having flown in the face of his folk roots, he once again blazed a different trail. By the mid seventies he re-emerged with this –'The Rolling Thunder Revue'- which, despite it's vastness, gives us a brief, unique and intimate snapshot into the life and times of this mercurial genius, the like of which we will never see again.

BOB DYLAN FREEWHEELIN HIS LIFE AND MUSIC

BOB DYLAN FREEWHEELIN HIS LIFE AND MUSIC

CHAPTER FOUR

CHAPTER FOUR

TRACK BY TRACK ANALYSIS

BOB DYLAN

1. 'You're No Good'

This was a song Dylan learned from its writer, Jesse Fuller, a West Coast singer. It comes across as a bit of a laugh, with an almost vaudeville atmosphere. You can hear Dylan stifling a giggle halfway through. What's odd is that this song leads an album of serious songs and doesn't really represent at all what's to come. His voice sounds high and young in this number, not really as it usually did. It makes the listener wonder if the producers wanted to tone down the album's harsh messages with a joke to begin with.

2. 'Talkin' New York'

Instantly, this is another world altogether, with a deep booming voice from Dylan and some cutting-edge lyrics for the time, exposing the bleaker side of city dwelling. This is the Dylan his fans came to love and worship, not the pastiche of a character the first song suggests. The song gives a great description of winter blues for a folk singer trawling the streets with his

guitar, winding up in Greenwich Village. He keeps the humour flowing with his story of being described as a hillbilly folk singer by the club owners and having to earn his living blowing harmonica. This style of storytelling would be one of Dylan's trademarks over the years.

3. 'My Time of Dyin''

This is the track on which he uses Suze Rotolo's lipstick holder to act as a capo while he plays some sweet blues and slide guitar. According to the liner notes, this was the first time he had come across this song, which shows his quick mastery of a new tune. His voice sweeps between blues and gospel with a nice gravel to it, certainly not the voice of a guy barely 20 years old.

4. 'Man of Constant Sorrow'

A traditional folk song from the southern mountains of America, which receives the Dylan treatment on guitar and harmonica, with his voice holding long wailing notes that almost echo the notes on his harp. Another quintessential Dylan song in its style and content, the sort of thing his purist fans always held dear.

5. 'Fixin' to Die'

The quality of Dylan's voice sounds even more raspy than usual, which suits the song perfectly. Almost touching on Tom Waits, this is the black blues voice of pain and poverty screaming out against injustice. Dylan pushes the song to a desperate level with his passionate rendition of the lyrics. Stunning.

6. 'Pretty Peggy-O'

A traditional Scottish song that Dylan does his best to infuse with some highland vigour, but not without coming unstuck once or twice, when it sounds a bit trite. Imagine a Scottish Piper with a Texan hat on and you should get a rough idea of this odd mix.

7. 'Highway 51'

The first of many down-the-road songs that Dylan's fans would love to listen to and take as reason enough to head out into the unknown. Great passion and variation in his delivery of the lyrics really add to the track, but again, the listener can sense he's treading water, and occasionally it just sounds too contrived.

8. 'Gospel Plow'

Some manic harmonica kicks off this up-tempo gospel tune; Dylan belts out the message with the zeal of a Southern preacher gone slightly mad.

9. 'Baby Let Me Follow You Down'

Dylan prefaces the song with its history of being written by Eric Von Schmidt, a great blues guitarist he had met on his travels. It almost sounds as if he's in a cafe giving a recital to a few friends, with the song's laid-back vibe and its tongue-in-cheek lyrics.

10. 'House of the Rising Sun'

Dylan learnt this well-known song from Dave Van Ronk, who was another of his musician friends around the Village in the early sixties. Van Ronk put him up a lot at his flat and helped to further his career considerably by introducing him to all the right people. In Dylan's hands this song gets a beautiful and personal treatment, with just his guitar and voice carrying its considerable weight. The recording is another example of Dylan giving some real passion to his performance, which more than makes up for any limitations.

11. 'Freight Train Blues'

This romps along as fast as Casey Jones on a sunny day, with about as much seriousness. The harmonica playing is representative of Dylan's style, and his long-held notes almost seem to parody himself. It's a lot of fun and was probably better live.

12. 'Song to Woody'

Dylan's great missive to his hero is a beautifully crafted song that displays fine finger-picking work and lyrically shows great promise. Of course, the style of playing reflects Guthrie's own attributes. The heart of the song is in the lyrics, and the story of the young man following in the elder's footsteps. One of his best early compositions.

13. 'See That My Grave Is Kept Clean'

Written by Blind Lemon Jefferson, this is a sad tale of disease among the Southern blacks and their fight for redemption. Dylan handles the tough subject with just the right amount of passion and restraint, showing a level of maturity that many wouldn't be able to mimic so well at his age.

THE FREEWHEELIN BOB DYLAN

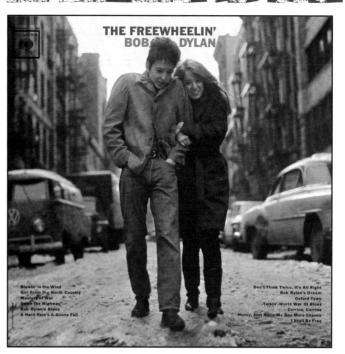

1. 'Blowin' In The Wind'

On the liner notes Dylan asserted, 'I still say that some of the biggest criminals are those that turn their heads away when they see wrong and know it's wrong. I'm only twenty years old and I know that there's been too many wars ... You people over 21 should know better. The first way to answer these questions in the song is by asking them. But lots of people have to first find the wind.'

Dylan was touted as the new spokesman of his generation, and at this early stage he didn't seem to have a problem with making grandiose claims. It wasn't long before he regretted this status and tried to shy away from being the people's voice. The production here, as on much of the album, is sparse, with just Dylan, his guitar, and harmonica. This helps to give the vocals more prominence, and there is little more engaging to the ear than just a voice and guitar.

2. 'Girl From The North Country'

This song had been hanging around Dylan's muse for about three years before he finally wrote it. He wrote, 'That often happens, I carry a song in my head for a long time and then it comes bursting out.' It is, in its simplest form, a love song, but there is a fine quality to the lyrics that allows the listeners to implant their own images. Dylan's lyrics tend to be visual; this is one of his strengths as a writer, painting pictures for his audience.

3. 'Masters of War'

Dylan wrote, 'I've never really written anything like that before. I don't sing songs which hope people will die, but I couldn't help it in this one.' The song is sort of strummed, with a rhythmic death-march feel to it, while the vocal pleads with some of the strongest lines Dylan will ever write. His indignation is clear and his sense of injustice was timely, considering the debacle of Vietnam that was developing and the frigidity of the Cold War. 'You're not worth the blood in your veins', which is another simple yet so effective line, one that would please any songwriter if it was their best effort.

4. 'Down the Highway'

Dylan speaks here for the wanderers and the lonesome blues musicians. He is clear in his opinions about the music, explaining, 'The way I think about the blues comes from what I learned from Big Joe Williams. The blues is more than something to sit at home and arrange. What made the real blues so great is that they were able to state all the problems they had, but at the same time, they were standing outside of them and could look at them.'

5. 'Bob Dylan's Blues'

This was supposedly a spontaneous composition, but it does give the sense that Dylan had a few of these lines already up his sleeve from many a cafe session. He explained, 'I start with an idea and then I feel what follows. Best way I can describe this one is that it's sort of like walking a side street. You gaze in and walk on.'

6. 'A Hard Rain's a-Gonna Fall'

The beauty of this song is that Dylan couches it as a conversation between a boy and his parents. This immediately gives it a personal angle that appeals to its listeners and shows that Dylan knew how to bring his audience in close. Its words are so classic it's hard to think of ways to describe its impact in the early sixties. Songs just hadn't really sounded so much like a bastard form of poetry, and their power was in that lyrical quality. Another Dylan masterpiece. 'Where the executioner's face is always hidden'.

7. 'Don't Think Twice, It's All Right'

On the liner notes, Dylan put his case for this beautiful love song. 'A lot of people make it a love song, slow and easy going', he wrote. 'But it isn't a love song. It's a statement that maybe you can say to make yourself feel better. It's as if you're talking to yourself. It's a hard song to sing. I can sing it sometimes but I ain't that good yet. I don't carry myself in the way that Big Joe Williams, Woody Guthrie, Leadbelly and Lightnin' Hopkins have carried themselves. I hope to be able to someday, but they're older people.'

Remarkably candid words from a young man; he went on to point out how music for these people was salvation, but for him, he still finds it hard to sleep at night.

8. 'Bob Dylan's Dream'

A great story song that carries the tale of Dylan's dream. It came initially out of a conversation he had with Oscar Brown Jr. in Greenwich Village. He explained that when he went to England and saw Martin McCarthy playing a song called 'Lord Franklin', it gave him the melody for the guitar.

9. 'Oxford Town'

This tells about the murder of two men under the Mississippi moon, a reference to another racial killing. Dylan passed it off as a song he learnt as a banjo tune, but put it to guitar.

10. 'Talking World War III Blues'

Another story song that tells the tale of Bob Dylan's nightmares, displaying an incisive world view of what would happen if World War Three ever happened. Again, he manages to make his approach so personal it's as if he's singing just for you, another of the talents he honed as a performer. A collection of fine lyrics makes this another masterpiece on an album that is full to the brim with them; it's awesome.

11. 'Corrina Corrina'

This is one of the songs for which Dylan has some backing, and he takes this traditional number to another place. Normally it lilts along like a love song should, but Dylan pushes it a bit faster and makes it more a statement than a love song.

12. 'Honey, Just Allow Me One More Chance'

As if to offset the dark thoughts contained in some of the album's songs, Dylan hams it up a bit here and manages to get across some humorous moments. This is much improved by some lively harmonica playing that really sets the song on another level. A lot of fun.

13. 'I Shall Be Free'

This is another of Dylan's off-the-cuff songs that displays his ability to rhyme on his feet, something learnt from doing numerous gigs. It's a nice way to round off the album, as it doesn't let the listener down, it ends on a high note, and leaves listeners wanting to return to side one and start the experience all over again. This is the clue to Dylan's albums; they are a journey and an experience we share with him, and he seems to know what his audience is pondering at the time.

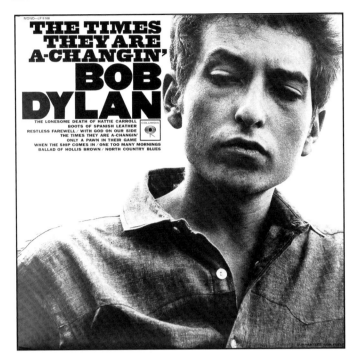

1. 'The Times They Are A-Changin' '

Dylan kicked off the album with the strongest track in many ways, stating the obvious in a melancholy diatribe. The mood is dour and stark, just like the black-and-white photo on the cover that depicts a rough young man looking downcast, with his hair shorn like a convict's. Whatever the vibe, the mastery of the lyrics and the beauty of the guitar work cannot be understressed. The song was actually written before Kennedy's assassination; it almost seems as if Dylan foresaw the changes.

2. 'Ballad of Hollis Brown'

Another minimal guitar piece with the quiet rant of Dylan's vocal on top. The picture he paints is of a terrible world where only damnation and pain roam the wilderness. This is so much heavier than the mood of the previous album it makes a different kind of a statement and adds a world-weary point of view.

3. 'With God on Our Side'

Another lament for the soldiers involved in routing the Indians in the early days of America. A sad tale told with a voice that seems to be tired and worn-out. Its nine verses almost add up to a history lesson.

4. 'One Too Many Mornings'

Another particularly quiet, downbeat song. It almost seems as if Dylan is trying to tell his audience something about himself with this collection of dour tunes, only accompanied by a slice of harmonica.

5. 'North Country Blues'

Dylan hosts the cause of the shipbuilders from the North who often died in the workplace, as it was such a tough environment. On the record, this is the last track on the first side, and it's possible to wonder who has the courage to flip it over and go through another five laments on side two. By far the most depressing side of Dylan to date, indicating his growing sense of personal dissatisfaction and his need to move on. Just about this time, the Beatles were making inroads into America, and Dylan began to see their harmonies and their energy as the new music toward which to lean.

6. 'Only a Pawn in Their Game'

Well, any hopes for a lighter side two were eclipsed in the first line, when the blood begins to flow. Like 'The Ballad of Hollis Brown', this song was derived from a newspaper report that Dylan had read. The only difference here was the colour of the plaintiff – white this time – Dylan acknowledging that the pain of the white trash was often just as keen as that of the black community.

7. 'Boots of Spanish Leather'

A slightly more melodic offering that would become a favourite of the fans, often requested at concerts. Dylan's voice at least attempts some singing, rather than the melancholic rant of the previous tunes. What really comes across is the eloquence of his lyrics within this love song, line after line delighting its listeners.

8. 'When the Ship Comes In'

Dylan almost broke into a run on this one, the guitar strumming along at a pace. His voice is more powerful and provocative. A fine bit of harmonica finishes off the track with some raised emotions. Dylan shows a fine mastery of melody in his singing, taking the lyrics up and down the scales at will.

9. 'The Lonesome Death of Hattie Carroll'

The sombre mood returns; the sorrowful voice laments another tale. This time it's about a black maid called Hattie Carroll, who was murdered by a white man named William Zanzinger, a high-flying landowner. In the end he only gets a six-month sentence for this atrocity, and Dylan voices his indignation that a black life is worth so little in the law courts. A great piece of social commentary, but along with the other songs on this album makes for some heavy listening.

10. 'Restless Farewell'

The mood continues without any accompaniment as Dylan closes this album of thoughtful observations with just his voice, guitar, and harmonica. In the final line of the song, Dylan seems to be saying goodbye to this period of his playing and stating that he's not just a pawn in his audience's palm. In amongst this, Dylan almost gives his fans an apology for what's to come and what's been done.

1. 'All I Really Want to Do'

This album was produced by Tom Wilson, and Dylan blamed him for the title and any other problems with it. To be sure, Dylan discovered more than ever that he was never going to be able to please all his fans. Many took an instant dislike to these songs. Compared to the songs in the previous album, 'All I Really Want to Do' is almost a comedy number, with Dylan purposely distorting his voice into a yodel every now and then.

2. 'Black Crow Blues'

Dylan surprised his fans by banging out a blues on the piano for this song. Again the mood is fairly light by comparison, perhaps fuelled by the copious amounts of red wine Dylan drank through the session. He summed up his new mood to Nat Hentoff by saying, 'Me, I don't want to write for people anymore.

You know – be a spokesman. From now on, I want to write from inside me.'

3. 'Spanish Harlem Incident'

A melodic guitar-strummed song that has some levity to it thanks to the energy of Dylan's performance.

4. 'Chimes of Freedom'

One of the best-known songs from the album, it retained some of his earlier songs' protest edge, satisfying some of the fans' need for such politics. The song became an anthem for freedom fighters the world over as they adjusted the words to fit their own injustices. A great melody in the vocal line keeps it alive and has the effect of drawing listeners closer to the performer. Perhaps its best aspect is the clarity of the vision worked through the lyrics, Dylan again demonstrating he's on a level of his own when it comes to writing songs that can last a lifetime and touch a generation.

5. 'I Shall Be Free, No 10'

This is almost a comedy number for Dylan, packed full of contemporary jokes and references. A nice touch is the use of his harmonica, which sounds about as jolly as it ever will, while he drawls with his voice to add to the comedic effect.

6. 'To Ramona'

The main love song on the album, although not the best known, as the emotional politics of 'Ballad in Plain D' overshadowed it. However, there are some beautifully constructed images and lyrics that make this a classic. Dylan's voice sounds warm and inviting as he draws each picture and verse with a soft brush. Lines like, 'Your cracked country lips I still want to kiss,' are appealing in their simple humility. The first side of the record draws sweetly to a close with this song and leaves a radically different impression from the sentiments at the end of side one on the previous album.

7. 'Motorpsycho Nitemare'

A light-hearted ramble through Dylan's imagination. This sounds like one of those off-the-cuff humorous songs that were popular in the folk cafes and clubs. For a change there's no harmonica on this one.

8. 'My Back Pages'

Dylan shows how he can impart melody to his lyrics on this laid-back view of his past, the melody he puts into the singing being perfect for the strident tone of his voice. The song contains the brilliant observation, picked up by many of his fans, 'I was so much older then / I'm younger than that now.'

9. 'I Don't Believe You'

A fine love song that has quite an unusual tune for him. It sounds upbeat, although not everything is roses in this relationship. 'Without any doubt she seems too far out'. At this line he broke into a small chuckle, which he hardly held back as he spilled into the next line.

10. 'Ballad in Plain D'

This song got the press, because it was later regretted by Dylan as one song he could have left on the notepad. Its two sisters are actually Suze Rotolo and her mother Carla, who took great offence at seeing her protection of her daughter immortalised in song.

11. 'It Ain't Me Babe'

Perhaps one of the most successful songs on this album and one of those that has lasted throughout the years as a favourite with the fans. Lord knows how many relationship break-ups this song has been the soundtrack for. It was certainly an emotion to which many men could relate, and perhaps that is why it's so enduring. Whatever the reasons, it was a fine song with which to end the album, and it's always good to make sure the final impression is a good one.

1. 'Subterranean Homesick Blues'

The album opens straight into the full-band sound with a song that would become a firm favourite with those fans who understood Dylan's need to move on. The song draws its inspiration from the famous 'Too Much Monkey Business' by Chuck Berry. It actually showed that Dylan could sound good at full tilt with a band, and it's a shame they ever held it against him, but such was the power of conservative convention in America.

2. 'She Belongs to Me'

A mellow treatment with the drums and lead guitar tucked away in the background. Flaunting some hauntingly strange lyrics, this is a fine love song, though not his most renowned.

3. 'Maggie's Farm'

A fine, rock-and-rolling number, with Dylan fronting the band with a vengeance while the guitars tinkle away contentedly in the background. Oddly, this would resurface many years later in England, when miners were realising that Maggie Thatcher wasn't going to put up with them any longer: 'I ain't gonna work on Maggie's Farm no more!'

4. 'Love Minus Zero / No Limit'

The band is definitely in the background in the production with this song, and it only makes all the fuss seem so ridiculous. A perfectly acceptable, chilled-out love song that really shouldn't harm anybody.

5. 'Outlaw Blues'

There's a bit more kick in this one with a stronger band backing, but it can in no way be said to take over Dylan's essential sound. A basic blues format with a jug band sound created among the musicians that works fairly well, though the song doesn't really go anywhere, tending to establish a rhythm and stick with it.

6. 'On the Road Again'

Dylan rocks it out in fine form with this somewhat lighthearted road song.

7. 'Bob Dylan's 115th Dream'

The first take dissolves into laughter as Dylan messes up the line. Take two has a full band in place and the song runs along like a young child in the summer. Dylan creates a real upbeat mood with his band, the harmonica, and the distinctly treble lead that rolls right through the song, all lifting the mood, while the lyrics are playfully rebellious and slightly taunting. At 6+ minutes it's almost double the usual length of a song and showed that Dylan was up for pushing the boundaries. Indeed, one song on side two would make 7+ minutes.

8. 'Mr. Tambourine Man'

The opening refrain is so deep in our consciousness it's almost like hearing an old friend speaking again. The song is a classic in its own right, though the Byrds were to make the most commercial success out of it with their version, which in my estimation, to be honest, isn't as good as this one. Still, the lighter pop feel they added to it was right for the teenage audience that was buying the records and the singles as the sixties progressed. As discussed above, the song is an amalgamation of the Mardi Gras and a Turkish tambourine.

9. 'Gates of Eden'

Side two of the record sees Dylan treating some songs, like this one, with the old solo troubadour touch. Why his folk purists couldn't have just enjoyed these few crumbs instead of rejecting the entire package is beyond me, but says more about the American temperament. 'The lonesome sparrow sings / There are no kings / Inside the Gates of Eden.'

10. 'It's All Right Ma (I'm Only Bleeding)'

A dark, sombre mood immediately grabs listeners as Dylan rants out a dismissive world view. This is a classic Dylan masterpiece that ought to have silenced any critics; his ability to deliver lyric after lyric in this complex picture is outstanding and the refrain, 'It's all right, Ma' is so common it brings the listener into the plot. At this time there was a deep sense of unease about the whole political situation, which this incredible song expressed.

11. 'It's All Over Now, Baby Blue'

One that would be a firm favourite with the fans at concerts for many years, this is another brilliant song with lyrics that will outlast Dylan's tenure on the planet. Its great use of a muted lead guitar to add melody to the vocal is a clever device to pretty up his voice, which shouts a bit. A firm favourite with bands all over the world who loved to sing the chorus, as it was something every guy could relate to at some point in his life. All in all, side two should have been enough to allay the folk purists, but that wasn't to be the case, as the next Newport festival would plainly demonstrate.

HIGHWAY 61 REVISITED

1. 'Like a Rolling Stone'

A momentous song by Dylan that only serves to confirm his awesome ability to write classic lyrics. Driven along by Al Kooper's Hammond organ, it sums up a light sixties sound. The best part of the song is that Dylan's voice finally sounds really at home with a full band backing. Instead of sounding a bit strident above a quiet guitar it cuts through the mix of a live band. It was released in August 1965 through CBS, whose execs must have come to see their boy as the golden goose.

2. 'Tombstone Blues'

A rocking blues that rattles along at full tilt, 'Tombstone Blues' comes alive with Dylan's lyrics, which never fail to surprise and delight. Mike Bloomfield's guitar really adds something to the whole sound of the track, and many other spots on the album. He seems to have the perfect blend of sound to enhance Dylan without taking anything away, and as soon as a lead break calls he jumps in faster that you can say B flat.

3. 'It Takes a Lot to Laugh, It Takes a Train to Cry'

A fantastic piano-led melody that lilts along like a slow boat down the Mississippi. Dylan drawls his lyrics, and there's a whole different vibe here to anything from the past; Dylan really sounds as if he's enjoying being part of a band. Before, it always seemed a bit like a case of Bob Dylan plus a band, but here he sits right in the mix and comes across as just another lead singer in a jug band.

4. 'From a Buick Six'

I have to admit that out of all Dylan's repertoire this is one of my favourite numbers. Why that is I'm not really sure, but something in the lyrics about 'if I fall down dying, she's bound to put a blanket on my bed', seemed to strike a chord with me. A fabulous collection of lyrics and a great melody. Yet again Dylan blows the lid off the roof of expectation.

5. 'Ballad of a Thin Man'

On the other hand this is one of Dylan's numbers that lacks some conviction in the lyrics. Supposedly based on an encounter with a reporter at the 1965 Newport festival, he comes across as a bit jaded and world-weary. The best part is the organ, which has a particularly haunting sound.

6. 'Queen Jane Approximately'

This track kicks off side two on the record with some stirring keys and a pleasant enough song, though Dylan delivers the lines in a way that doesn't really make the most of the situation. However, some feel this was his intention with this song, to give it a weary sense of regret and desperation. It was actually composed while he was on tour in England.

7. 'Highway 61 Revisited'

Highway 61 is the major road that runs south from where Dylan was raised in Duluth to along the Mississippi River to New Orleans. The song itself is one of Dylan's comedy rants. It's not bad, but hardly of a level with some of his other more serious compositions. Still, he may have felt there was only so much social commentary you could have before you had to give in to something a little more laid back.

8. 'Just Like Tom Thumb's Blues'

Yet another world-weary sounding song, with Dylan delivering his lyrics through a smokescreen of tired resignation; it's as if he was suffering some weird depression. The song has plenty of drug references in it, and the basic premise is that the song discusses the negative effects of coming down from amphetamines. Certainly the vocal and the stripped-bare backing all add to the sense that it's four in the morning and the last line has gone.

9. 'Desolation Row'

At over 11 minutes this song rewrote the rulebooks on the length of tunes on albums, and probably paved the way for a whole plethora of musical genres. Where would psychedelic or progressive rock be without tracks of 10 minutes and longer? Far from being as depressing as the title sounds, the song has a decidedly upbeat production to it, with some brilliant lead

guitar on a nylon-strung instrument, which gives the song a Spanish twist of lime to it. As it progresses we are introduced to a fine array of characters from every section of life, all juxtaposed against a post-apocalyptic world. Mike Bloomfield saves the listener from any sense of the song going on too long, as his lead guitar work flows like a stream endlessly evolving this way and that. Dylan must have enjoyed the thrill of wondering what folks like the Beatles and the Rolling Stones would make of his new offering. Sure enough, their next albums would all contain longer numbers, eventually reaching the lengths of Sgt Pepper's Lonely Hearts Band.

1. 'Rainy Day Women #12 & 35'

Released in August 1966, this track summed up the mood amongst young people, who were increasingly taking drugs and experimenting with all sorts of alternative lifestyles. Dylan was again right on the money. The track is full of humour and would perhaps have been better placed at the end of a side rather than the beginning. Dylan was breaking every convention on this one, and perhaps that is why he listed it in this order. This was also the first double album to come out, beating Frank Zappa, who was next in line with his double extravaganza Freak Out, by a couple of months.

2. 'Pledging My Time'

A fine blues number performed with a full band sound and some strident harmonica leading the solo. The lyrics are throwaway, but add to the sense of irreverence on the album.

3. 'Visions of Johanna'

Dylan trawls through his imagination, coming up with so many different images and ideas it's hard to know exactly where he's going with it all. He sounds like the old master talking to the children about his vision of epiphany. One of the sweetest additions to the track is the organ, which has a rolling Hammond sound that fills the background so perfectly you can spend a lot of time just listening to the way it works the spaces in the vocal.

4. 'One of Us Must Know'

An interesting depiction of Dylan's imagination cast against a bleak background. He gives out the impression that he is unable to get close to people, but it leaves the question of how much that was of his own making. The band almost creates a wall of sound behind it all.

5. 'I Want You'

One of the more successful melodies, with the band sounding like a formidable cohesive force. What is unusual about the song is the depth of Dylan's emotion and his revealing a need for his partner. Up to this point, Dylan had never been one to give in to love's dominance, but he comes across as more mature and more at home with these complex emotions. The song is uplifting, and certainly has one of the prettiest refrains Dylan had sung during this period. Wayne Moss played the beautiful guitar intro.

6. 'Memphis Blues Again'

A soft rock ballad that sweeps along on the crest of the organ. Dylan's story about riding the railroad is enchanting, full of the usual crazy characters that come partly from his imagination and no doubt partly from the denizens of the America he used to frequent. His voice sounds clear and strong, perhaps reflecting a happier lifestyle with less stress and more quality time spent with his family.

7. 'Leopard-Skin Pill-Box Hat'

The theory goes that this song refers to a wild socialite and somewhat crazy walking piece of art called Edie Sedgwick. She and Dylan used to hang out in the old days around the Big Apple and beyond, enjoying some of the crazier side of life, but there is never any direct admission from Dylan that this is the case, so we just have to rely on the reports that she wore a leopard-skin hat and leave it at that. This is a mid-paced, rocking number that has the band

kicking out some fine riffs and giving Dylan a garage type of sound. Dylan often made them record after only the briefest run-through of the chord structure, sometimes not even running through to the end, so that they would never know just when it was going to come to an end. This did have the effect of keeping everybody on their toes, but it meant that they didn't have the luxury of coming up with melodies and harmonies, they just had to magic it together on the spot. Brilliant.

8. 'Just Like a Woman'

If this was the only decent song on the whole album it would still be worth buying just for that. A fabulous portrayal of a woman, again some believe to be Edie Sedgwick, but one to whom Dylan gives such pathos and poignancy that the song lives on in the listener's mind long after it has finished. A classic set of Dylan lyrics set off with an awesome chorus, songs like this really mark him out as a talent way beyond the ordinary.

9. 'Most Likely You Go Your Way (And I'll Go Mine)'

Something of a rhythm and blues ballad that has a real band feel to it, with the electric lead guitar providing a riff-based melody. A good story accompanies the lyrics, with his voice sounding a bit jaded and husky, perhaps he'd been smoking some good-quality grass at the time, as was often the case for Dylan during this era. It helped keep him a bit chilled out when the pressure built up, and he was certainly under a lot of strain at the time.

10. 'Temporary Like Achilles'

This is a much more laid-back number with a three in the morning feel to it. Some good piano makes a change as the lead instrument on top of the jangling guitars. Dylan's voice sounds exhausted, but maybe that's the intention. Even the harmonica playing is lacklustre, tending to come across as a bit of a filler on the album, compared to some of the genius evident elsewhere. At one point he almost lapses into the melody of a line from 'Like a Rolling Stone'. Was Dylan finally running thin on ideas?

11. 'Absolutely Sweet Marie'

Beach Boys meets the Monkees is about the level of this light-hearted, summery romp. It's led to a degree by the organ, which has that typical sixties sound, it echoes some of his past work, except for the brief key change in the middle eight, which comes as a surprise; it's something Dylan had never used before to lift a song. The harmonica in this lead break tries its best to sound like a guitar running through note after note. Nothing to rewrite the rulebooks but pleasant enough.

12. '4th Time Around'

A really nice change of pace and treatment here, as a nylon-strung guitar takes over the lead spot. The song has a sleepy feel without being downbeat. The arpeggio background melodies are so pretty it's worth listening to the song for those alone. At one point it sounds as if Dylan is pinching a bit of a Donovan song to bolster up the melody. Again, this isn't on a par with songs like 'Just Like a Woman', but it's perfectly suited to filling side three of a double album.

13. 'Obviously 5 Believers'

Almost something of a hard-rock Deep Purple riff here. This one has echoes of 'From a Buick Six' in the melody; it really sounds like Dylan has stretched himself, and this might have been much better as a tight single album without the weaker tracks like this one that don't add much to his repertoire and reflect previous releases.

14. 'Sad Eyed Lady of the Lowlands'

This song takes up the entire length of side four, which at almost 11? minutes long it doesn't warrant. Needless to say, nobody had ever done that before, either. This album was produced by Bob Johnston, and the great atmosphere on this song must in some way be down to his understanding of what Dylan was out to achieve. None of Dylan's producers ever seemed to get the praise others did for working with lesser stars, but part of the problem was that Dylan always grabbed the headlines and the other partners on his projects have often been forgotten.

The organ has a hymn-like quality with a bass edge to its sound, while Dylan chants his lyrics clearly above the metronomic drumming. This was the first track the session musicians recorded with Dylan, and none of them had the faintest idea it was going to last as long as it did, which is why every now and then it sounds as if they're bringing it to a climax, but Dylan just drags out another verse, and on they go into the night. This was done in one take, which makes it even more extraordinary and proves Dylan's ability to get the best out of anybody who collaborated with him.

JOHN WESLEY HARDING

1. 'John Wesley Harding'

The album was released in February 1968, though most of the work had been done in 1967. The first thing that strikes the listener is that Dylan's voice sounds slightly different from before, a bit more fragile. Was this due to his accident, or just a change of tack? The song drifts along sweetly enough but doesn't really go anywhere other than the harmonica break, with no main chorus to back it up. Dylan himself would call this record the first Biblical rock album.

2. 'As I Went Out One Morning'

A small vignette of some mystical lady that may indeed have come from the Bible or a parable. Great bass guitar really sets off the bottom end of this song. It's one of the first times Dylan had let the instrument out of the bag.

3. 'I Dreamed I Saw St Augustine'

No way to avoid the religious reference on this one. It's a pleasant enough song, but perhaps better off in a church service.

4. 'All Along the Watchtower'

It would take Jimi Hendrix to immortalise this song with his incredible version that led to many others attempting it, too. It's hard to listen to the muted version by Dylan without hearing Hendrix's screaming guitar, but what comes over are the superb lyrics.

5. 'The Ballad of Frankie Lee and Judas Priest'

A fine story line related with minimal backing, the bass being prevalent again, warming up the bottom end. Notable in another way for giving the rock band Judas Priest their name. A song with a clear moral to it.

6. 'Drifter's Escape'

This is the most upbeat number on side one, but there's nothing here that Dylan hasn't covered before in other songs lamenting the fate of the poor.

7. 'Dear Landlord'

Another song that would be made far more famous by its rendition by Joe Cocker, who put more into one line of the vocal than Dylan could ever hope to achieve with his voice, certainly not at its best during this era. The piano leads this one for a change, but again comparing Chris Stainton's version with Joe Cocker leaves no comparison. If Dylan had copied this from Cocker, the version would have been panned as a pathetic effort by comparison; it's just as well he wrote the original. It does go to show that Dylan left room for interpretation and often under produced songs like this one.

8. 'I Am a Lonesome Hobo'

Sitting in his mansion on a probable stash of millions in cash makes this a bit far-fetched for some by Dylan; his days as a couch sleeper and hitchhiker were long gone and this tends to sound a bit hypocritical as a result. Some of the lines again have melodies that have surfaced in earlier songs. It seems Dylan was spreading his jam thinner and thinner with each album.

9. 'I Pity the Poor Immigrant'

This might suffer from the same ailment as the song above. Dylan's voice sounds decidedly weird on such a quiet song that has such a quiet backing there's nothing to disguise his odd tonal range in short a dour song with a dire vocal.

10. 'The Wicked Messenger'

Another Biblical tale of woe and sin, this is one of those songs when Dylan has played his harmonica too close to the microphone, and it gives it a slightly distorted treble edge which isn't the best of tones on the ear.

11. 'Down Along the Cove'

This sounds like a nice, jazzy blues-club number, cruising along at a fair rate of knots. It has a simple rock format based on a 12-bar blues. His voice at least sounds a bit better and has more inflection to it, but it's the same old harp again, starting to wear a bit thin.

12. 'I'll Be Your Baby Tonight'

Yet again a song that fared better in the hands of artists who could do the vocal some justice. Not to say that Dylan didn't have his style, but when great singers handle this song they can really give every word the power it needs. However, we cannot deny that he had written another masterpiece that would be sung all over the world for decades to come, so perhaps we shouldn't be so down on the guy. After all, that must have been some knock on his head when he fell off his bike to come up with this as an album.

NASHVILLE SKYLINE

1. 'Girl from the North Country'

Judging from the fine atmosphere on this recording, it would have been good to have a bit more of the session with Johnny Cash. The only downside is that they ought to have worked out the chorus before they launched into the tape. A fine example of two men who haven't a clue when the other is going to come in or where the accent on the syllable comes. Painful at times.

2. 'Nashville Skyline Rag'

A bit of finger-picking from Dylan on this up-tempo ragtime. Perhaps it was most startling for being a straight instrumental, not something Dylan had done before. Needless to say, the session musicians bring it to life.

3. 'To Be Alone with You'

A studio outtake starts this one: 'Is it running, Bob?' A song that many artists covered with great success, as it was a song that suited a vocal that could belt it out as sadly Dylan never could.

4. 'I Threw It All Away'

A lament that drags its heels with a murky production and a dour vocal that sounds like it's got too much reverb on it. It might have been better if he'd thrown this one away. The problem was that by now Dylan was such a huge star that nobody had the guts to tell him when he was producing absolute tripe.

5. 'Peggy Day'

This is almost a fifties sounding number, with its production and in particular its guitar sound. It wasn't the most exciting or earth-shattering of his songs.

6. 'Lay Lady Lay'

Clapton's version makes Dylan's sound as if it was underplayed, but he gets one of the best vocals of the record, although in a style that he rarely used, almost that of a crooner.

7. 'One More Night'

A country and western number. That's all I can bring myself to say. The best bit is the steel guitar and when it finally ends.

8. 'Tell Me That Isn't True'

Dylan's deep voice continues on this one, but lyrically this is child's play compared to his past compositions.

9. 'Country Pie'

An infectious piano boogie gets this one off to a flying start. A great little rocker, but no outstanding moments.

10. 'Tonight I'll Be Staying Here With You'

A mid-range middle-of-the-road ballad.

BOB DYLAN FREEWHEELIN HIS LIFE AND MUSIC